T0197061

PERSISTENCE
HAS GREAT GAIN

Persistence Has Great Gain

JOYCELYN DANKWA

authorHOUSE®

AuthorHouse™
1663 Liberty Drive
Bloomington, IN 47403
www.authorhouse.com
Phone: 1-800-839-8640

Published by AuthorHouse   09/29/2012

ISBN: 978-1-4772-3076-3 (sc)
ISBN: 978-1-4772-3077-0 (e)

Library of Congress Control Number: 2012917291

Any people depicted in stock imagery provided by Thinkstock are models, and such images are being used for illustrative purposes only.
Certain stock imagery © Thinkstock.

This book is printed on acid-free paper.

Because of the dynamic nature of the Internet, any web addresses or links contained in this book may have changed since publication and may no longer be valid. The views expressed in this work are solely those of the author and do not necessarily reflect the views of the publisher, and the publisher hereby disclaims any responsibility for them.

DEDICATION

I dedicate this book to God who has put His spirit upon me and anointed me to preach the good news to the poor. He has sent me to bind the broken hearted, to proclaim freedom for the captives and release prisoners from darkness, to proclaim the year of the Lord's favour . . . May His Name be praised forever. Amen

PREFACE

The motivation for this book is drawn from a personal experience. I know there are many women (and men) out there who are faced with the unexpected common phenomena of separation and divorce that has suddenly bedeviled the face of Christianity. Many who as a result of different circumstances have taken to ungodly lifestyles, many who have backslidden, many who have taken decisions and possibly many that are even contemplating suicide, I want to use this book to encourage you not to give up and to encourage you to persist. If you persist you will overtake and recover all.

I got married at a tender age and life was full of promises, I was happy, excited, born again and full of life. God also blessed our marriage with a wonderful son. All of a sudden like the title of one of Chinua Achebe's books—' *Things Were no longer at Ease'* and eventually '*Things fell Apart because the center could no longer hold.*' Before I could imagine what was happening to me my first marriage broke up.

I thought my whole world had collapsed. Apart from the emotional trauma and unexpected bleak future that I was suddenly thrown into the lost of properties we had acquired together during the marriage. I was left with a staggering debt of over £10,000 to pay; this happened during 2000-2001 in the expensive city of London. The experience of David in Ziglag[1] was a child's play compared to what I faced. I cried my heart out. How will I cope? Who will be a father to our son whom he had abandoned and left? What do I do next? I was troubled, shattered and scattered. To say it was a tough time was to lack the appropriate word. Then I remembered the words of Robert Schuller 'Tough times do not last only tough people do.' Following on the example of David I decided to encourage myself in the Lord and move on with my life. It was difficult but I put my life together. I decided not to marry again but focus on my calling and serve God. I knew I had a calling in my life so with a lot of intensive prayers God directed me to go to bible school, which I successfully completed. I was ordained as an Evangelist in Christ Apostolic Church.

God also called me into missionary work, which gave birth to Shepherd Fold Ministries. This ministry is focused on looking after widows, orphans and the poor and needy in the society, isn't this what God called the true gospel[2]?

Though faced with a lot of sexual temptations the Lord kept me holy, there was no man in my life during all this time that I was a single parent.

However as I was praying one night in Feb 2009 I heard a voice informing me that by April 2009, there would be a man in my life. I stopped the prayer and said, 'God that is not what I am praying for and let us not go there; how can it be?, the interval was very short. However has God not said His ways are not our ways, and that his thoughts are far from ours? In April 2009, I met my husband and to the glory of God we had a beautiful wedding in 1ˢᵗ August 2009 the same year. Believe me; he is a wonderful man, the man God sent to wipe away my sorrows. It was not easy for those nine years, I had to face financial difficulties, loneliness, insult, abuse, reproach, disgrace, name it. I looked to the cross and lay my burden under the feet of Christ. Psalm 105:4 *Look to the Lord and His strength; seek His face always*; this passage meant so much to me that it became *my motto.* You would never find me or see me anywhere except the house of God. Persistence is a great gain. At the appointed time God made things beautiful for me[3]. The thrust of this book is from Luke 18:1-8, where the importunate woman persisted until she had her breakthrough. Dear reader God will make all things beautiful for you. It is time for your break through. Reading this book will surely catapult you to your desired divine destiny.

Vatican Humor

After getting all of Pope Benedict's luggage loaded into the limo (and he doesn't travel light), the driver notices the Pope is still standing on the curb.

'Excuse me, Your Holiness,' says the driver, 'Would you please take your seat so we can leave?'

'Well, to tell you the truth,' says the Pope, 'they never let me drive at the Vatican when I was a cardinal, and I'd really like to drive today.'

'I'm sorry, Your Holiness, but I cannot let you do that. I'd lose my job! What if something should happen?' protests the driver, wishing he'd never gone to work that morning.

'Who's going to tell?' says the Pope with a smile.

Reluctantly, the driver gets in the back as the Pope climbs in behind the wheel. The driver quickly regrets his decision when, after exiting the airport, the Pontiff floors it, accelerating the limo to 205 kph. (Remember, the Pope is German.)

'Please slow down, Your Holiness!' pleads the worried driver, but the Pope keeps the pedal to the metal until they hear sirens.

'Oh, dear God, I'm going to lose my license—and my job!' moans the driver.

The Pope pulls over and rolls down the window as the cop approaches, the cop takes one look at him, goes back to his motorcycle, and gets on the radio.

'I need to talk to the Chief,' he says to the dispatcher.

The Chief gets on the radio and the cop tells him that he's stopped a limo going 155 kph.

'So bust him,' says the Chief.

'I don't think we want to do that, he's really important,' says the cop.

The Chief exclaims, 'all the more reason!'

'No, I mean really important,' says the cop with a bit of persistence.

The Chief then asks, 'Who do you have there, the mayor?' Cop: 'Bigger.'

Chief: 'A senator?' Cop: 'Bigger.'

Chief: 'The Prime Minister?' Cop: 'Bigger.'

'Well,' says the Chief, 'who is it?' Cop: 'I think it's God!'

The Chief is even more puzzled and curious, 'What makes you think it's God?'

Cop: 'His chauffeur is the Pope!'

CHAPTER ONE

PERSISTENCE WHAT IS IT?

(What is wrong with us?)

> "Failure is only postponed success as long as courage 'coaches' ambition. The habit of persistence is the habit of victory."
>
> —Herbert Kaufman

But those who hope in the LORD will renew their strength. They will soar on wings like eagles; they will run and not grow weary, they will walk and not be faint—Isaiah 40:31

ALSO [Jesus] told them a parable to the effect that they ought always to pray and not to turn into cowards (faint, lose heart, and give up). He said, in a certain city there was a judge who neither reverenced and feared God nor respected or considered man. And there was a widow in that city who kept coming to him and saying, Protect and defend and give me justice against my adversary. And for a time he would not; but later he said to himself, Though I have neither reverence or fear for God nor respect or consideration for man, Yet because this widow continues to bother me, I will defend and protect and avenge her, lest she give me intolerable annoyance and wear me out by her continual coming or/at the last she come and rail on me or/assault me or/strangle me. Then the Lord said, Listen to what the unjust judge says! And will not [our just] God defend and protect and avenge His elect (His chosen ones), who cry to Him day and night? Will He defer them and delay help on their behalf? I tell you, He will defend and protect and avenge them speedily. However, when the Son of Man comes, will He find persistence in] faith on the earth Lk 18:1-8 AMP

Then Jesus said to them, "Suppose you have a friend, and you go to him at midnight and say, 'Friend, lend me three loaves of bread; ⁶ a friend of mine on a journey has come to me, and I have no food to offer him.' ⁷ And suppose the one inside answers, 'Don't bother me. The door is already locked, and my children and I are in bed. I can't get up and give you anything.' ⁸ I tell you, even though he will not get up and give you the bread because of friendship, yet because of your shameless audacity[e] he will surely get up and give you as much as you need. Lk 11:5-7

There are similar stories and experiences comparable to the parable which Jesus gave in this instance. One of them is this: A man hired a labourer to dig a well for him. Half payment was made until the job was finished.

As they were digging the hole, they met a rock so they could not finish the job. The man called someone else, after many attempts, they could not break the rock. After a while in frustration they left. As soon as they left another man watching who was privy to what they were looking for but saw their shallow mindedness, quickly continued the digging, guess what? With a little labour he was able to penetrate the rock.

In the book *Think and Grow Rich* by Napoleon Hill, the author narrated a similar story. He wrote about a man who had a mining company in California. After a while, the raw material he was using for this material supposedly 'dried up'. In frustration; he sold the equipment cheaply to another company. As soon as the new company took over; they dug further than the previous owner and discovered a massive deposit of the same raw material. When the former owner of the company learned had what happened, he was taught a big lesson that persistence works. He went on to become an insurance sales agent. He wrote, "There is no potential client that I introduce my product to that did not say 'NO' initially." But from the experience he had from his failed mining company he knew that if only he dug deeper he will make sales. With vigour and persistence he became a millionaire insurer.

What is a parable?

One of the distinguished features of the teaching ministry of Jesus was His use of parables. About one-third of His recorded teachings were parables. A parable has been defined as "a metaphor or simile, drawn from nature or common life, arresting the hearer by its vividness or strangeness and leaving the mind in sufficient doubt about its precise application to tease it into active thought". Simply put, parables are comparisons or illustrations of spiritual truths with familiar and common life events. In a parable, the visible is used to explain the invisible, the simple to express the complex, the unknown to expose the unknown and the temporal to expound the eternal. But the use of parables by our Lord Jesus Christ had another unique dimension. While He used parables to reveal spiritual truths to earnest and sincere seekers (as the woman in this parable of importunity), He also used them to hide truth from curious and uncommitted skeptics, especially the hard hearted religious bigots (as the judge in this case). I want to believe that God used this parable to unearth the very important truth about persistence and how persistence is not only desirable but why it is probable. You will learn that life is a parable including yours!

Drive through Syndrome

The issue of persistence is an important key to our psyche in this age and this drive through generation. A lot of development has pushed us to a frenzied state that if care is not taken vocabularies like steadfastness, persistent, perseverance, and patience will soon disappear from our world. We have become victims of our environment. You get to a washroom, whether at the airports or hotels, corporate and residential places all you have to use are laser controls to open the tap. There is no time to manually turn taps any more. You just tap a knob to get your hands dried up, who has time for towels? To watch your flat screen plasma TV, a remote control can readily do this for you, because there is no need to even take a step. Imagine the increasing *drive through* inventions. *Tim Hortons* <u>Drive Through</u>, *McDonalds* <u>Drive Through</u>. *KFC* <u>Drive Through</u>. Pharmacies <u>Drive Through</u>. You cannot think of the *fast* food business without thinking of drive throughs in any of its outlets. Did you notice the word *fast* in the last statement? The type of food that people eat nowadays is fast food, no wonder there are so many health issues relating to the junk food that we consume which has led to a decrease in mortality. Nobody has the time to cook good meals and the commercial world has hijacked our appetite drive. I remember one of my Italian teachers in 1985 commenting on this fast life style saying 'you live fast, die young and leave a beautiful corpse.' Nobody has time to enter the bank and queue any more, first it was ATM machines that gave you access to banking 24/7. Now with the Cash shop drive through you just have to stay in your car press some buttons and numbers and your banking is done. The other day I saw a Laundromat drive through; I asked myself where are we rushing to? This drive through mentality has crept into the church such that all you have is drive through members (congregants). People show up today they are gone after three months. Members are no longer looking for miracles they are expecting magic. The back door is getting wider than the entrance door. The drive through mentality is so entrenched in Christiandom that it has permeated virtually all facets. Take marital issues. Gone are the days of courtship, what you have is dating, after three months to one year the marriage is consummate. Nobody takes the patience to find out who they are intending to marry. There as many dating and match making sites. The Internet with all the advantages has also been abused. People can easily deceive you as to where they are writing from and who is writing. A woman was lamenting the other on day on *CNN* about how a purported suitor duped her. Having divorced before (part of the impatient syndrome clause) she could not wait to look for a proper husband so she launched onto the Internet, advertised herself as a woman looking for a young man to marry. A woman capitalized on it and replied her using a fictitious name and also used the picture of a dead soldier in Iraq! She kept making fictitious, ridiculous and pretentious financial demands on the woman who needed a husband. "I miss you a lot', she wrote. "I need money to persuade my superiors to release me so that I can come and see you!" The whole story leaked out when the parents of the dead soldier found out that some people posted the picture of their late son on some websites as someone looking for a wife!

It is not only impatience in the selection process that is worrisome but the divorce rate. I heard that in Canada, on the streets of Toronto there are some companies that capitalize on this lack of perseverance; they make posters and adverts tagged "Quick Divorce for $299". They are not bothered about what the consequences of divorce will have both on parents and children, as long as someone can fill up their purse with some quick money. The impatience has crept into the lives of young students in Africa resulting in them not wanting to study. People cheat in exams to gain admission into tertiary institutions. They consider studying as an unnecessary waste of time. Forgetting that knowledge acquired and applied is power. In the western world among the blacks in the Diaspora, the dropout rate has increased phenomenally, simply because students are not willing to pay the price of studying. This cankerworm of *drive through* has permeated the society at large that everybody wants a *drive through* to riches. The materialistic society we have today, sadly, is an off shoot of *drive through* mentality. A business that is registered today must have a breakeven tomorrow. Even the *Prosperity* message and the *mega church* syndrome are all driven by the *drive through* mentality syndrome. A church planted today wants to have thousands of followers. There is nothing wrong with that if that church is *converting* souls through genuine soul winning and other spiritual exercises as opposed to diverting souls and stealing members from nearby existing churches. It is a drive through mentality that makes converts of three years and students of seminaries to call themselves Bishops, General Overseers and Apostles. In the light of the above it is important not only to revisit the issue of persistence being a great gain and a virtue that is needed and should be cultivated but to really take time to define what persistence is.

Persistence—what it is

To be persistent is to have uncommon determination to follow through what you believe God has called you to do. It is to develop the spirit of finishing. It is to have a determination not to fall by the way side. Persistence is to develop the spirit of doggedness. To be pushy. Persistence is the art of being diligent and resolute in pursuing a notable course. Persistence is synonymous with developing the attitude of endurance, patience. Persistence is a fruit of the spirit. The spirit that enables one to cross from patience to longsuffering without knowing. For the Christian it is to remain faithful till you receive the call to leave this world and relocate to heaven. The synonyms of persistence include but are not limited to endurance, patience, staying in power, survival, stamina, fortitude, continued existence, the act of persevering; continued patient effort and the quality of one who perseveres. Persistence is recognizing that there are challenges and hurdles to be crossed before life's visions are realized. That is the origin of the opium, 'no cross no crown.' That is what Jesus our Lord and savior went through; the scripture testifies 'having endured the cross'. Major dictionaries define persistence "as the art of persisting in or remaining constant to a purpose, idea or task in spite of obstacles."

Perseverance means strengthening of resolve. It is one of the vital principles of success. You must have heard the saying, "Keep knocking on the door, someone will surely open it." That means, if you want to open the doors of opportunities, you need to be determined enough. This is possible only if you persevere with courage and enthusiasm. The woman we shall be looking at in this book whose stories we read in the synoptic gospel of Luke persisted. Persistence is a determined skill that the leaders of this world possess in abundance. Persistence is probably the single most common quality of high achievers. To persist is to refuse to give up despite obstacles, excuses and exhaustion. Athletes, footballers and boxers refuse to give up, they keep training despite pain, injury, long hours and exhaustion. Why?, because they have a goal, a purpose, a vision, and the victory is worth it, every bit of the blood, sweat and tears it took them to get to the top.

At this juncture, let us look at some bible characters and see how they can help us understand perseverance. Perseverance is the goal that made it easy so that for thirteen years Joseph was kept from age seventeen to thirty from the day his brothers de-robed him as the colourful son of Jacob till Pharaoh re-robed him as the Prime Minister of Egypt. Persistence is the key word that prevailed in the life of David, the eighth born of Jesse who became the life king of Israel. It was persistence that help him wait for three levels of ordination in his father's house, in Hebron over Judah and in Jerusalem before becoming king over the entire nation of Israel. He fought the longest war with his boss in scripture (I Sam 18-26). He had opportunities to kill Saul and became an instant king but he had this phrase in his mouth "how can I touch the anointed of the Lord." Persistence for ten years of unrepentant attendance of Shiloh is what gave the privilege to Hannah to produce a replacement for the revered priest in the land of Israel by the name of Eli when the Lord gave her Samuel who became the last judge of Israel. Persistence even with initial faulty steps is what gave Sarah, Isaac the child of laughter. Persistence is what will bring laughter to your life[4]. *Through faith also Sara herself received strength to conceive seed, and was delivered of a child when she was past age, because she judged him faithful who had promised*

It was persistence that enabled Noah to preach for 120 years without a convert and he was not discouraged. Noah was building an ark for a flood when he had never seen rain but dew and yet he persisted.

Before Paul wrote about the crown awaiting him he wrote about challenges:

I have fought the good fight, I have finished the race, I have kept the faith. [8] Now there is in store for me the crown of righteousness, which the Lord, the righteous Judge, will award to me on that day—and not only to me, but also to all who have longed for his appearing.

The challenges: *Are they Hebrews? So am I. Are they Israelites? So am I. Are they Abraham's descendants? So am I. [23] Are they servants of Christ? (I am out of my mind to talk like this.) I am more. I have worked much harder, been in prison more frequently, been flogged more severely, and been exposed to death again and again. [24] Five times I received from the Jews the forty lashes minus one. [25] Three times I was beaten with rods, once I was pelted with stones, three times I was shipwrecked, I spent a night and a day in the open sea, [26] I have been constantly on the move. I have been in danger from rivers, in danger from bandits, in danger from my fellow Jews, in danger from Gentiles; in danger in the city, in danger in the country, in danger at sea; and in danger from false believers. ²⁷ I have labored and toiled and have often gone without sleep; I have known hunger and thirst and have often gone without food; I have been cold and naked. ²⁸ Besides everything else, I face daily the pressure of my concern for all the churches. ²⁹ Who is weak, and I do not feel weak? Who is led into sin, and I do not inwardly burn? II Corinthian 11:22-28*

You probably have heard about Ruth, one of the daughters in-law of Naomi, she saw no reason to wait for Naomi to be a point of comfort for her anymore, in the words of Naomi 'if I should conceive and bear a son today you will not be able to wait.' Lo and behold Ruth waited and Oprah could not. Ruth ended up as an ancestral mother of the Lord Jesus Christ. She got married to Boaz, Boaz gave birth to Obed, who gave birth to Jesse and Jesse was the great grandfather of great David.

Friend, I think it is persistence on the part of God that made him to wait after creation for four millennia before sending his only begotten Son to the world to save humanity.

It was persistence that made God to wait for you till you gave your life to Christ. Do you remember how many sermons you heard that had no meaning to you? Do you remember all the night vigils you attended? As far as you were concerned the pastor was just talking to himself then. Can you remember all the abortions you committed and God was waiting for you to repent and be saved? *You should remember all the time you pretended to be in the choir and you were sleeping around with the women and yet you were the chorus leader! Remember all you did on Saturday night before coming to church on Sunday and God was still waiting. Can you remember the time you were involved and dancing with masquerades? Can you remember when you were an armed robber? Can you remember when you were into drugs and gangs? Today you are now addressed as "Man of God", "Woman of virtue", "Mother-in Israel", "Anointed servant of the Most High" and a practicing Christian just because God was faithful to his own word* the true word *"The Lord is not slow in keeping his promise, as some understand slowness. Instead he is patient with you, not wanting anyone to perish, but everyone to come to repentance[5]"*

Persistence is what makes the farmer to wait for three to four months before harvesting food crops and many more years to harvest a cash crop. It is persistence that makes a rejoicing newly conceived woman to wait for nine months before bringing forth her God—given child. It is persistence that makes an elephant to wait for 22 months in pregnancy to bring to the world a baby elephant. Even nature understands patience and perseverance that is why summer does not struggle with winter neither does spring fight with autumn (fall).

Have you heard of the likes of Thomas Edison, the electricity inventor, Henry Ford the automobile giant, Alexander Bell the telephone guru and the Wright Brothers who made flying in the air possible. These inventors did not carry out those works in a hurry. It was not a *drive through* mentality that got them to that prestigious position, it was the spirit of persistence that shot them to world fame and people who made life livable for their generation and others after them. Nothing tangible in life has ever been achieved without persistence. As a mother I know what I went through in travail and labour to give birth to my son like other mothers I was between life and death. It was not an easy process pushing a human being from the womb to the world. But to the glory of God after I endured that moment I have quickly forgotten that pain because my joy is everlasting and is momentarily rekindled any time I see my son. Persistence is a virtue. Persistence has its rewards. Persistence is a great gain. Jesus said men "ought always to pray and not faint." Paul said "let us not be weary in well doing for in due season we shall reap if we faint not"

CHAPTER TWO

WHY PERSEVERE?

The following quotation is from Jesus Christ but for emphasis and better understanding it is translated from different bible translations

[22]And ye shall be hated of all men for my name's sake: but he that <u>endureth to the end</u> shall be saved. KJV

And ye shall be in hate to all men for my name; <u>but he that shall dwell still into the end</u>, shall be made safe. [And ye shall be in hatred to all men for my name; forsooth he that shall continue till into the end, shall be safe Wicklliffe

And you will be hated by all for My name's sake, but he <u>who perseveres and endures to the end</u> will be saved [from spiritual disease and death in the world to come]. Amplified

Everyone will hate you because of me. But anyone <u>who stands firm to the end</u> will be saved. NIV

Everyone will hate you because you are true to me. But the person, <u>who keeps on being true </u>to me until the end, will be saved. World wide English version

[22]Everyone will hate you because of me. But if you <u>remain faithful</u> until the end, you will be saved. Contemporary English version

I Will Persist Until I Succeed[1]!

I will persist until I succeed.

In the Orient young bulls are tested for the fight arena in a certain manner. Each is brought to the ring and allowed to attack a picador who pricks them with a lance. The bravery of each bull is then rated with care according to the number of times he demonstrates his willingness to charge in spite of the sting of the blade. Henceforth will I recognize that each day I am tested by life in like manner. If I persist, if I continue to charge forward, I will succeed.

I will persist until I succeed.

I was not brought into this world to live a life of defeat, nor does failure flow in my veins. I am not a sheep waiting to be prodded by my shepherd. I am a lion and I refuse to talk, to walk, to sleep with the sheep. I will not hear those who weep and complain, for their disease is contagious. Let them join the sheep. In a similar vein, I am not a chicken I am an eagle. As the lion rules the bush so the eagle rules the air. Dominion is my portion. The slaughterhouse of failure is not my destiny.

I will persist until I succeed.

The prizes of life are at the end of each journey, not near the beginning; and it is not given to me to know how many steps are necessary in order to reach my goal. Failure I may still encounter at the thousandth step, yet success hides behind the next bend in the road. Never will I know how close it lies unless I turn the corner.

Always will I take another step. If that is to no avail I will take another, and yet another. In truth one step at a time is not too difficult.

I will persist until I succeed.

Henceforth, I will consider each day's effort as but one blow of my blade against a mighty oak. The first blow may not cause a tremor in the wood, or the second, or the third. Each blow, of itself, may be trifling, and seem of no consequence. Yet from childish swipes the oak will eventually tumble. So it will be with my efforts of today.

I will be likened to the rain drop which washes away the mountain; the ant who devours a tiger; the star which brightens the earth; the slave who builds a pyramid. I will build my castle one brick at a time for I know that small attempts, repeated, will complete any undertaking.

I will persist until I succeed.

I will never consider defeat and I will remove from my vocabulary such words and phrases as quit, cannot, unable, impossible, out of the question, improbable, failure, unworkable, hopeless, and retreat; for they are the words of fools. I will avoid despair but if this disease of the mind should infect me then I will work on in despair. I will toil and I will endure. I will ignore the obstacles at my feet and keep my eyes on the goals above my head, for I know that where dry desert ends, green grass grows.

I will persist until I succeed.

I will remember the ancient law of averages and I will bend it to my good. I will persist with knowledge that each failure will increase my chance of success at the next attempt. Each nay I hear will bring me closer to the sound of yes. Each frown I meet only prepares me for the smile to come. Each misfortune I encounter will carry in it the seed of tomorrow's good luck. I must have the night to appreciate the day. I must fail often to succeed only once.

I will persist until I succeed.

I will try, and try, and try again. I will consider each obstacle as a mere detour to my goal and a challenge to my profession. I will persist and develop my skills as the mariner develops his, by learning to ride out the wrath of each storm.

I will persist until I succeed.

Henceforth, I will learn and apply another secret of those who excel in their work. When each day is ended, not regarding whether it has been a success or failure, I will attempt to achieve one more sale. When my thoughts beckon my tired body homeward I will resist the temptation to depart. I will try again. I will make one more attempt to close with victory, and if that fails I will make another. Never will I allow any day to end with a failure. Thus will I plant the seed of tomorrow's success and gain an insurmountable advantage over those who cease their labor at a prescribed time. When other cease their struggle, then mine will begin, and my harvest will be full.

I will persist until I succeed.

Nor will I allow yesterday's success to lull me into today's complacency, for this is the great foundation of failure. I will forget the happenings of the day that is gone, whether they were good or bad, and greet the new sun with confidence that this will be the best day of my life.

So long as there is breath in me, that long will I persist. For now I know one of the greatest principles of success; if I persist long enough I will win.

Have you started a job and abandoned it? Have you seen someone who started school and quitted. Are you familiar with people who have either separated or divorced their spouse? Do you know of a single mum or single dad? They all have one denominator, they started something they did not finish it.

To be frank with you it is very easy to start anything. In many nations people register companies daily but it may interest you to know that many do not even leave the drawing board. Many start churches and it never goes anywhere. It is easy to get married, to have children, to register a business, to secure admission to school, matriculation is easy and desirable but what will get you a job is convocation, it is not easy to finish. Unfortunately it is those who finish and finish well that usually win the prize. When I was growing up I heard people say 'Olympics is not to win but to participate'. It is now that I realize that people really win medals and become instant celebrities with a lot of money to spend and a lot of endorsement awaiting them.

Let us look at five reasons why you need to persevere.

Keep on keeping on

Quitters never win, winners never quit. One of my pastor friends in Canada once narrated this story to me. He said a woman came to his house one day to show appreciation for her daughter that had just graduated from college. She said the woman had two children and the two were schooling in different schools in

Canada. The elder one graduated with distinction. As the celebration was going on, the mother said—Pastor I appreciate what you did for my daughter but it is my son that I really want to thank you for. The mother said when she brought her son from Nigeria to Canada she had the hope that the boy would do well in Canada. Unknown to her the boy faced all manners of challenges in the Canadian college that he eventually left the college and went back to Nigeria. "I was just eating with my husband one day when this boy showed up in Nigeria." She narrated to my Pastor.

Is this your ghost or something? The mother queried her son when she saw him in Nigeria all of a sudden.

"It is not my ghost. But I am tired of schooling in Canada; as a matter of fact I do not want to go to school anymore." The young man said.

The parents were disturbed and troubled. That was their only son. They asked him the question, "Son, how can we help you". He just shrugged his shoulders. After a long pause he said "whatever" and left the room. The parents went ahead and looked for another university for him in Nigeria. After some months, the same boy came back and told the parents he did not want to go back to school any more. After a long discussion he decided he wanted to go back to Canada, but not to the university where he had been studying and he didn't want to do the course he had been studying. The parents reluctantly took him back to Canada. That weekend they visited my pastor's church. The mother was surprised after the service when the boy came with all the excitement the mother had not seen in the past nine months from his child.

"Mum I got it." The young man said

"What did you get" the mother asked with a lot of curiosity in her voice and face.

"Did you not hear the pastor, he said the quitter never wins and the winner never quits" the boy retorted with greater excitement in his voice and his face aglow.

"I still do not get what you are saying, son" the mother explained.

"Well I believe that man's sermon was meant for me, I got a rhema word. Quitters never win, winners never quit. I am not a quitter and I am a winner. For the past nine months I have quitted school. Right now I am going back." the young man explained.

"Okay. We shall go to your school tomorrow as scheduled and we shall get your transcript and apply to another university so that you will continue your education." The mother said with some hesitation and guided joy.

The boy put the card clearly on the table. "Mother," he said. "I am not a quitter I am a winner. I am going back to school tomorrow. I do not need to change college neither do I need to change my discipline. If others can graduate in that college I can. If others can read my course and graduate I can. I am not a quitter I am a winner." The boy replied. The mother was extremely happy. The boy went back to school and has since been doing well with a remarkable performance. The mother shared the testimony with my pastor. The reason you must persevere is that if you quit you are the loser, if you persist you are the gainer. The question one needs to ask is 'why are many Christians quitters instead of those who soar like eagles in our time?' Because they are not flying high enough to catch the powerful winds of God's Spirit. They have not taken advantage of their eagle attributes, and they aren't behaving like eagles at all but more like the canaries, buzzards and peacocks of the world. I like the sayings of Amos Dada the convener of International Gathering of Eagles conference around the world—' I am not a chicken, I am an eagle I must soar' Read more from his book[5].

There hath no temptation taken you but such as is common to man: but God is faithful, who will not suffer you to be tempted above that ye are able; but will with the temptation also make a way to escape, that ye may be able to bear it.

The Road Map.

There is always movement in life. Human beings are dynamic. It is a great movement to move from the Stone Age to the industrial revolution into the sophisticated age we have found ourselves. Has the journey been easy? I guess not. When I think of the climatic regions and the Stone Age when there was no electricity I marvel. The man, Thomas Edison credited to have invented electricity was known to have performed over ten thousand experiments before achieving that feat. Yet human beings persisted and waited for his invention. Once there was a time in the university when we had giant rooms filled with giant computers and cards were punched to interpret data. Today that has gone; the world is filled with laptops, I-phones, I-pads and small sized gadgets which are more sophisticated and process information faster. Once there were times when you needed a map before you could move from one destination to another, it gravitated to map-quest and today it is called the Global Positioning System (GPS). Before the telephone was invented we had telegraphs. Before DVDs were invented we had VHS. Before we had the tape player we had gramophones! All devices and systems have one thing in common there is a road map to get you to a destination. The reason for you to persist is that there is a road. There is a distance from one point in life to the other. If life is so cheap and easy and there was no need for a journey then there will be no impediment on the way, the issue of persistence will not arise. Isaiah described how difficult roads can be. *Every valley shall be exalted, and every mountain and hill shall be made low: and the crooked shall be made straight, and the rough places plain[6]*

The journey of life is long. You will need to persist because there are waves on the sea, turbulence in the air and the roads are full of hazards. Only the persistent one can go over them.. May you be one of them.

The length of the road may be different, some may be shorter than the others or longer than the others and many times full of mountains, valleys, windstorms, snowstorms, hurricanes, volcanic eruptions but all these can only delay the human journey but cannot deny it. If the pursuer is determined to persevere. Delay is surely not denial.

3. Success is what you need

If wishes were horses, beggars will ride. The reason why you need to persist is that you have a vision of what you want to be. You have a place you are going in life. You have a purpose and assignment you are pursuing. You have a marriage to keep. You have children to raise. You have a ministry to accomplish. You have a degree or certificate to obtain. You have a business to start, company to run and to make profit. You are talented and equipped for something great. Success is what you need. What you need is not failure. What you want is not divorce; what you want is a good marriage. That widowed woman in our story wanted to be *avenged of her adversary*. Probably her adversary had made up his or her mind to eliminate her. She desperately wanted to live. She had a goal to live. You have a goal to not only live but to live well. You have a goal not only to live but to live a prosperous life not a life saturated with lack, want and poverty. You don't just want a marriage that is endured you want a marriage that is fruitful, blissful and enjoyable. You do not just want children but godly children. You do not just want a husband but a godly spouse. The story was told by Pastor E. Adeboye of a woman who was praying desperately for a husband.

One day a man came to her. Then she looked at the man closely and saw the wretchedness of the man, she then knelt down with her hand in a praying position and offered a prayer of protest to the Lord "O Lord I asked you for a husband, not a thing!" Nobody wants inferior stuff, Lever brothers PLC has a productivity slogan: Produce results not reasons. What you want is lemonade not a just lemon. What you need is financial freedom not financial bondage. What you need is prosperity not poverty. What you want is a baby that you will raise unto God like Hannah not to tell stories of how many miscarriages you have had without one baby in your house. If there were no miscarriages this scripture would not have existed: *and none will miscarry or be barren in your land. I will give you a full life span[7]*. Your goal is not to miscarry but to have children. Because you had one miscarriage or the other is not a conclusion that you are barren, you go back to the mating room. What you desire is not just to be a Pastor but to depopulate hell and populate heaven. What you are craving for is to carry out the great commission not to produce a failure card of omissions. Persistence in pursuit of this is one of the credible routes to succeed in life that is why you must persist. If you fail to persist you will be cast to the dungeon of failure. Persistence is the road map to success.

Show me a man, who persisted, I will show you a man who succeeded

Show me a man who refused to give up I will show you a man who became a champion.

Show me a man who saw a test as a stepping stone, I will show you a man who has a testimony.

Show me a man who is not overcome by trials I will show you a triumphant conqueror

No Room for excuses (Prayer is not cheap)

The words of E.M Bounds are worth revisiting. "Energy, courage and perseverance must back the prayers that heaven respects and God hears . . . . Persistence is made up of intensity, perseverance and patience . . . . Faith functions in connection with prayer and of course, has its inseparable association with persistence. *But the latter quality drives the prayer to the believing point.*" Bounds goes on to say "The absolute necessity of persistent prayer is plainly stated in the Word of God and needs to be stated and restated today . . . . Love of ease, spiritual laziness, and religious indifference all operate against this type of petitioning."

You must come to the realization that God is the only one who can help you get off. It's time to lose the pride and the self efficiency. It's time to be like those desperate ones in the Bible whose faith and persistence healed them.

Prayer is not cheap but is a necessity for us as Christians. Part of the significance of the parable we shall be considering in this book is about persistence in prayer. That is what Jesus was teaching. If praying was easy there would not have been a necessity for Jesus

*to lay this emphasis. Luke the physician has eleven unique parables two of them teach about importunity. The parable of the friend in Luke chapter eleven from verses five through eight is to equally stress that. We are in a generation of Christians that make excuses over the issue of prayer. Jesus also described these excuse givers i*n Luke 14, Jesus told a parable about three men who were invited to a great feast but who all declined the invitation, this is a parable that illustrates this increasing non-involvement in spiritual exercises through flimsy excuses. Before I return to the story of these three men; let me tell you two stories of how ridiculous people can be in giving excuses. The other day I went to the mall to pick up a family for fellowship. As I was about to drive off, I noticed a man by the passenger side. Though it was winter time and cold I managed to wind down the window glass to attend to this man. "I am homeless can you help me with some change for a meal" he said matter of factly." My passenger told him we had no change. However, I ignored him and reached to my car pigeon hole and came out with some coins. "Look here have some change" and I stretched out the money. By the time he collected the money and was about to move away I realised that this is a western country, unlike most of the African nations, they have welfare packages and shelters, so there was no reason for him to be begging for money. I asked him why he was homeless in a country like this, when there are many shelters begging you to come in. Without blinking an eye he said "I was once in the shelter and they stole my property!" He walked away. My friend and I busted into laughter. This showed how ridiculous people can chicken out from persistence. How could somebody find a reason not to stay in the shelter and walk about in the street begging? Will his property be safer in the streets? What precious properties does he have which would have been stolen in the shelter that necessitates his being homeless?

I was told of another story of what happened in Nigeria at a time. The MTN telecommunication company organised a promotional event. The company organised a marathon race for Africans with the first price at a whooping fifty thousand dollars. People came from all over Africa. Thousands of youths and adults trooped out to run the race. At the end of the race a young man from Kenya won. The media then went around interviewing people that did not win. One of them was a young Nigerian. "Sir, why did you not win this race?" he was asked. "The Nigeria government did not provide infrastructure" was the reply! What infrastructure do you need to prepare for a marathon? No roads in Nigeria for you to practice on? The issue of excuses is major in making many not to reach their life goals.

Let us go back to the three men from the scriptures. These men could humorously be appropriately named: Retail Tom "I have bought a piece of ground and I must need go and see it"; Farmer Brown—"I have bought five yoke of oxen, and I go to prove them" and Handsome Harry—I have married a wife, and therefore I cannot come." (Luke 14:18-20)

Each man conveniently "excused" himself by citing respective responsibilities concerning merchandise, maintenance and marriage. While these were all legitimate activities, they replaced the most important event, an event that Christ applied to himself and participation in the eternal kingdom of God—Luke 14:15. As the writer pondered this parable, he thought about the increasing reticence of professing believers to become engaged in the following three vital Scriptural endeavours: prayer, faith and love. Note that the land, the animals and the wife are not running away, but they all missed the great opportunity. Particularly in the western world we give so many excuses for a prayerless attitude.

When you fail to persist in prayer you miss out on revelation. When you miss out on revelation you miss out on direction, for it is in the place of prayer that direction is given. When you miss out in the place of revelation you miss out in the place of mysteries. Jesus had no reason to pray as man in God and God in man but to demonstrate the need for persistence in prayer he spent his life in prayers, night and day and in fasting. Live with no excuses, be thorough going and through. Love with no regrets for love is a winner any day any time. When life gives you one hundred reasons to cry, show life by God's grace that you have one thousand reasons to smile. Keep your smile on for God is on your side. You will surely get the best laugh that will last I am sure. Be encouraged.

5. The bones will rise again.

Understanding God's input is critical to the ultimate victory you deserve in life. Be assured that God makes us brave when we are afraid, makes us strong when we are weak, but most of all, he teaches us to hold onto him when things keep falling. There is no hopeless or helpless situation when God is involved. His intervention which is based on his absolute power turns defeat to victory, frustrations to fulfillment. Note that the dry bones shall rise again Trust God and weep not wipe your face. The departure of Elijah is to get the mantle to Elisha. The departure of Jesus is to make the Holy Spirit available and universal. You will rise again. You must persist, the wrapper packaging many times is deceitful. Who can imagine what happened in this scenario:

The hand of the LORD was on me, and he brought me out by the Spirit of the LORD and set me in the middle of a valley; it was full of bones. ² He led me back and forth among them, and I saw a great many bones on the floor of the valley, bones that were very dry. ³ He asked me, "Son of man, can these bones live?"

Many times when we find ourselves climbing a life mountain as Ezekiel was climbing, we often hear the question. "How did I get here" "Why am I here?" "What sort of hopeless situation is this." Now you can answer some of those questions. It is God that led you there not the devil. The Spirit of God not demons, it is God's direction not witches and wizards. You are there because God wants you to see him in power. God wants you to learn a lesson in your life. One of my favorite verses in the scripture is:

Praise be to the God and Father of our Lord Jesus Christ, the Father of compassion and the God of all comfort, ⁴ who comforts us in all our troubles, so that we can comfort those in any trouble with the comfort we ourselves receive from God. ⁵ For just as we share abundantly in the sufferings of Christ, so also our comfort abounds through Christ. ⁶ If we are distressed, it is for your comfort and salvation; if we are comforted, it is for your comfort, which produces in you patient endurance of the same sufferings we suffer. ⁷ And our hope for you is firm, because we know that just as you share in our sufferings, so also you share in our comfort. II Cor 1:3-7.

You have to be persistent because you are in the University of Dry Bones(UDB) to earn a degree in *Transformology.* God wants you to learn how he can transform literal physical dry bones to a literal person, becoming an army!

Then he said to me, "Prophesy to the breath; prophesy, son of man, and say to it, 'This is what the Sovereign LORD says: Come, breath, from the four winds and breathe into these slain, that they may live.'" ¹⁰ So I prophesied as he commanded me, and breath entered them; they came to life and stood up on their feet—a vast army.

You are going through that experience because God wants you to learn how to prophesy. You can't do this until you see dry bones become a vast army. When Ezekiel stated prophesying nothing was happening only "rattling noise" Your life is a school. You have Dry Bone Course (DBC) 100, note that he got to 400 level before he graduated. In life course you don't even graduate that fast. It is because you don't graduate so fast that is why you need to develop an attitude of patience, perseverance and persistence. There are so many dropouts in the University of Dry Bones you do not need to add yourself to them.

Paul says every Christian needs a degree in 'Transformology' so that they can perform live assignments.

Do not be conformed to this world (this age), [fashioned after and adapted to its external, superficial customs], but be transformed (changed) by the [entire] renewal of your mind [by its new ideals and its new attitude], so that you may prove [for yourselves] what is the good and acceptable and perfect will of God, even the thing which is good and acceptable and perfect [in His sight for you]. Romans 12:2 Amp

Reader you are down today you will rise tomorrow, your business has collapsed today it will be running tomorrow, you are a spinster today you will be a bride tomorrow and also double as a mother. You are sick today you will be healthy tomorrow. All you need is persistence, it works. Dry bones shall leave again. In the later chapters, we shall learn more about *how* to be persistent

CHAPTER THREE

DISSECTING THE FACTS

It is good for us to understand the terms of the contract before we sign it. The fine prints of contract papers are the most dangerous if one is not careful. The sales men of this world most times pressure us to make decisions, and many times we regret our decisions. Nothing takes God off guard. Remember his plan for you began at the beginning of time. When we feel rushed and hurried to make a decision that is not firmly planted on God's word, God is probably not the one speaking. Nowhere in the scripture does God tell us to rush into a decision, On the contrary, he patiently and persistently gives us clarity before obedience. If you feel an overwhelming urge to act spontaneously when you do not understand what is going on, pull in the reins. A friend wanted to purchase a new car when he was financially struggling. A pushy salesman was trying to rush him into a decision. The deal that the salesman was giving him was a good one, however he felt uneasy and uncertain.

Even though he knew he could miss out on the deal, he felt uneasy and anxious about it and he walked away. A few weeks later he was given a car by an anonymous donor.

Let us look at the bold and fine prints of the parable our Jesus gave us about the widow and the judge so that we can have a better grasp and better application of the story to our lives. The Bible unlike the other books is a living word. Many people read the Bible but few meditate on it. Until you meditate on the word you cannot get health and wellness for your soul and life from it. God said to Joshua[1] "if you read and mediate on the law and observe to do what is therein, then you will make your ways prosperous and have good success.' Jesus said the truth you know is what will set you free. The truth you know, understand and apply is what will set you free. Knowledge is information. Information is very good but information is not enough, it has to be processed, well understood. Understanding is comprehension. If you have an electrical appliance and you do not know how to use it the appliance is of no use to you. The story was told of how an Indian man who came to New York in the past century saw a washing machine and discovered how easy it washes cloth. He was very delighted. He bought one and took it back to India. On getting there he did not know how to operate it. Eventually he was putting fowls there for incubation purposes! Understanding is key but understanding is still inferior to wisdom. Wisdom is the application of knowledge. For example there is nothing worse than a medical doctor who is smoking! He has information about the danger of it, he understood the implications and many times teaches it to his patients but he cannot apply that knowledge to his life. I am hoping that you will have information through this book, get understanding through this book and have the courage to apply wisdom to your life.

Let us go back to the main story of this book like a biologist let us dissect the principal characters.

Then Jesus told his disciples a parable to show them that they should always pray and not give up. ² He said: "In a certain town there was not a judge who feared God nor cared what people thought. ³ And there was a widow in that town who kept coming to him with the plea, 'Grant me justice against my adversary.' ⁴ "For some time he refused. But finally he said to himself, 'Even though I don't fear God or care what people think, ⁵ yet because this widow keeps bothering me, I will see that she gets justice, so that she won't eventually come and attack me!" ⁶ And the Lord said, "Listen to what the unjust judge says. ⁷ And will not God bring about justice for his chosen ones, who cry out to him day and night? Will he keep putting them off? ⁸ I tell you, he will see that they get justice, and quickly. However, when the Son of Man comes, will he find faith on the earth,(Lk 18:1-8)

From the last statement Jesus was asking if He will meet faith on earth. Will I meet people on earth who will persevere in their faith and benefit from it? Will I meet people who will not give up cheaply because of challenges they are facing in their life curriculum? It is to make sure you have faith and you keep faith that this parable was given, by the King of Kings and the Lord of Lords. We shall discuss more about faith but it is important to bear in mind what the author of Hebrew wrote about persistence and faith. *And what more shall I say? I do not have time to tell about Gideon, Barak, Samson and Jephthah, about David and Samuel and the prophets, [33] who through faith conquered kingdoms, administered justice, and gained what was promised; who shut the mouths of lions, [34] quenched the fury of the flames, and escaped the edge of the sword; whose weakness was turned to strength; and who became powerful in battle and routed foreign armies. [35] Women received back their dead, raised to life again. There were others who were tortured, refusing to be released so that they might gain an even better resurrection. [36] Some faced jeers and flogging, and even chains and imprisonment. [37] They were put to death by stoning;[e] they were sawed in two; they were killed by the sword. They went about in sheepskins and goatskins, destitute, persecuted and mistreated— [38] the world was not worthy of them. They wandered in deserts and mountains, living in caves and in holes in the ground[2].*

The Judge

The first character in the parable was a ***judge*** who never feared nor cared what people, thought! A judge is a professional, an appointed or elected magistrate who is tasked with promoting justice by presiding in a fair and impartial manner over court proceedings and deciding questions of law or discretion in which advocates present their cases for a resolution of the issues by a jury or the judge. Socrates[3] once said, "Four things belong to judge: To hear courteously, to answer wisely, to consider soberly and to decide impartially." Deciding impartially means, to adhere strictly to and not divert from a standard of what has been determined as right, true or lawful. To be completely devoid of favor for or prejudice against one side more than the other. Being just means more than being fair. It means to demonstrate humanity; to feel compassion for and understanding of the concerns of the litigants as persons; a recognition that achieving justice to the litigants before you is more than slavish allegiance to dictates of mechanical jurisprudence.

The judge in this parable has an adjective saying *"he that neither feared God nor cared what people thought."* Isn't that what you and I have faced all our life? People who you thought will assist you but are the ones to backstab you. Husbands who have promised heaven on earth during courtship especially on the wedding day and early marriage then suddenly turned out to be serious wife abusers and vice versa. People, who are stubbornly wicked, callous, without regard for human feelings and consideration. Listen to how Paul describes them:

The Spirit clearly says that in later times some will abandon the faith and follow deceiving spirits and things taught by demons. ² Such teachings come through hypocritical liars, whose consciences have been seared as with a hot iron. I Tim 4 :1-2

Paul is not through yet, read more:

But mark this: There will be terrible times in the last days. ² People will be lovers of themselves, lovers of money, boastful, proud, abusive, disobedient to their parents, ungrateful, unholy, ³ without love, unforgiving, slanderous, without self-control, brutal, not lovers of the good, ⁴ treacherous, rash, conceited, lovers of pleasure rather than lovers of God— ⁵ having a form of godliness but denying its power II Tim 3:1-5

Will these kinds of people disappear from the face of the earth? I do not think so. If they were existing when the Bible was being written, I think they have really multiplied on the surface of the earth. You will always find birds flying over your head but you cannot prevent that, however you can deny them the luxury of building a nest on your head.

Even though America is well advanced in technology, America cannot calm a natural storm. On perennial basis when the hurricane season is approaching some states or cities make effort to evacuate and relocate people to minimize human and material losses because they cannot prevent the storm.

The first approach therefore in perseverance is to know or locate a man who can handle chaos, storm, pandemonium and such categories of troubles. There is someone who will say 'Peace' and the storm and wind will obey. Today, Jesus is speaking peace to every storm in your life. Peace could also be the absence of danger. Isaiah 26:3 says 'if only you can fix your heart on Christ, nothing can threaten you.' How safe are you?

Isaiah 9:6 says Jesus is the Prince of Peace. Peace could mean any of these: It could be the absence of war. Proverbs 16:7 says pleasing God forces your enemies to settle with you. Peace can also be the absence of a storm. You can fight human enemies but a storm is difficult to fight.

Knowing that man and locating him is not enough. I Peter 5:7 says "Cast all your anxiety on him because he cares for you." How do I cast my cares? This is what the widow taught all of us who will care to learn. This will be deliberated upon later in this book.

The Judges Options

Let us see the possibilities of the judge's actions towards this widow and the challenges she might have faced.

The Judge did not ignore the woman :

This judge is in a position to ignore this woman. Despite the widow's importunity the judge can refuse to answer. In all facets of life no matter how you feel about yourself and others, the other person always has a choice. Choice first and consequences later. Remember Esther and Mordecai—if you keep quite at a time like this God will raise up help from another source[4]. Remember the triumphant entry event. The religious leaders said Jesus should warn the children from praising him. Jesus said if they keep quiet, stones will arise and speak. It is very good that this judge did not ignore the woman. Nevertheless, let me put you in the position of the judge and let us assume you did not respond positively what do you think will happen? God will raise help from another source for the woman. The Judge teaches us that whatever is in your capacity to do, go ahead and carry it out.

Judge refused to insult the Woman.

The judge has the choice to insult this woman. The judge is in a position to deride her or look at her position and make fun of her. He could say. 'Woman, why are you troubling me, did I kill your husband? Am I your adversary?' The Psalmist[5] started by saying "*It is a blessed person who does not sit in the company of mockers'* Nicodemus an erudite lawyer came to Jesus at night seeking a way to enter God's kingdom, he was by all means older in age than Jesus. Nicodemus could not come during the day but at night. Jesus was in position to insult him but he quietly ceased the opportunity to teach him and the entre human race how to be born again. The judge teaches us how no matter highly placed you are do not underestimate the other person. The fact that the other person has a need today does not mean that will always be the case. The fact that you are the boss today does not mean you will be forever. No condition is permanent. The Judge does not fear God or man, but was surely considerate, civil, well behaved and non—judgmental. How do you treat your neighbour? How do you treat your subordinates? How do you treat the under privilege in the society? Many people in public office in our generation insult the general intelligence of the people they are to hold in trust or swore an oath to protect. They legislate oppressive laws, increase taxes they promised never to increase, loot the treasury dry by misappropriation of funds. It is in our generation that judges are re-defining marriages, permitting same sex marriages. Some as 'Judges' in the church also follow the conventional judges in the society to impose gay personnel as Bishops this is an unimaginable insult upon the congregant. The judge in question refused to insult the widow. I guess the judge realised he was not paid with public funds to insult the citizenry.

Judge did not abuse the widow

The judge did not abuse this widow. You can argue that the judge had no reason to delay. You can argue that the judge may have had an ulterior motive for his answer because of what he stated-(So that this woman does not wear me out) but he refused to abuse the widow. What is an abuse? Abuse can be physical, sexual, emotional or verbal; it is intimidation or manipulation of another person or an intrusion into another's psyche; the purpose is to control another person. It is generally a long term pattern of behaviour or it can be a specific short term interaction and this can be labelled abusive. Recently the following categories have been included in the definitions of abusive behaviour: social, economic, intellectual and spiritual. The judge could easily have abused her sexually. Make a just demand of her and exploit her situation. Since abuse generally tends to happen to people in a weaker position or to those who are willing to be accommodating. The judge could deal with her by asking his servants, security, dogs to chase her away from his presence. Abuse cuts across all social categories and classes. It occurs in well educated high income areas and in low income working class areas; it happens in all races and religions. It can occur in families, extended families, in neighbourhoods, <u>schools</u>, <u>churches</u>, and community groups. Both men and women can be abusive and it can occur in virtually all age groups. The old can abuse the young and the <u>young can abuse the old</u>. While standards are different in various cultures, it occurs in virtually all countries as well.

I believe God is not just teaching us the power of prayer in this parable or limiting us to importunity lessons, Jesus is using this opportunity to teach human behaviour. Abuse has become a major phenomena in our generation. Jesus is saying it need not be so. It is ridiculous and abominable for a father to sexually abuse his daughter whether she is a biological daughter, step daughter or spiritual daughter. Why do we have so much divorce in our generation if it is not due to all manners of abusive life styles that we exhibit. There is so much shortage of tolerance, patience and long suffering in our mental and practical relationships. What gives you the impression that beating your wife will make her to be a better-behaved wife or mother or vice versa? You are the judge in your house, office, church and neighbourhood. Many widows will come to you with one request or the other, please stop abusing them.

Judge did not reject the widow

Her appearance was not revealed in the discourse. However for a poor widow to show up in the chamber of a wicked judge we can imagine her dressing, apparently nothing spectacular. She could have had a bad odour due to poor finances but the judge did not reject her. *Bishop* Oyedepo[7] *said "The Worth of a man is not in his dress, it is in his address"* The judge may be genuinely occupied by the cases of many people of higher social status who probably came in their cars and limousines and were sophisticatedly dressed in their designer wears, this judge was not dissuaded by those physical issues-what was ringing in his ears was, the request of this woman-*avenge me of my adversary.* He was probably thinking if 'I avoid this woman's case today, the headline in the news paper the following day may be informing the public about the death of this woman.' That was too risky for this judge. He may not fear man or God but he surely was not going to have blood on his hands by rejecting this widow! You might have been a victim of rejection before and that is why you are hesitant in pursuing your life goals, I have good news for you Jesus has suffered every rejection for you. Listen to how Isaiah[8] and John write about what he has done in this prophecy and its fulfilment.

He was despised and rejected by mankind, a man of suffering, and familiar with pain.

Like one from whom people hide their faces he was despised, and we held him in low esteem

The true light that gives light to everyone was coming into the world. [10] He was in the world, and though the world was made through him, the world did not recognize him. [11] He came to that which was his own, but his own did not receive him. [12] Yet to all who did receive him, to those who believed in his name, he gave the right to become children of God— [13] children born not of natural descent, nor of human decision or a husband's will, but born of God

Jesus was not portraying the judge as a good man in this parable but as being wicked. He however uses the opportunity to tell humanity about his kingdom and personality, if this wicked man will not reject you, be sure enough, God will not reject you. Are you facing one rejection today or another, come to the man who has suffered rejection for you on the cross of Calvary. If the wicked judge did not reject this woman Jesus will not reject you. He says *though your sins be as scarlet he will make it as white as wool. Though it be red like crimson he will make it as white as snow[9]*. Growing up in Africa I did not understand the in-depth meaning of that scripture because I had never seen snow. After seeing snow especially in Canada, I know what Jesus has done by dying on the cross.

Many have committed suicide today because they felt rejected. I know a couple that was having a very rough marriage. The husband just knew that his wife was a very sad person. The woman never disclosed why she was always sad. The husband eventually invited a man of God to minister to both of them. It was in the process that this woman revealed the genesis of her negative behaviour and sadness. In Africa, and some other parts of the world including the Jews, if a woman becomes a widow and the late husband has a younger or elder brother they will compel both of them to marry. This tradition is practiced whether the woman or man likes it or not. The wife of this couple suffered a similar fate. Her mother was given to a man to marry after the death of her husband. The man did not want her mother but he was forced to marry her. The wife in this story is the unfortunate daughter her widowed mother had for her new husband. The man rejected this girl. He refused to treat her as his own child. This lady could not get over this childhood and adulthood rejection until that man of God ministered deliverance to her. Deliverance is yours today. Listen to Jesus conclusion—*And will not God bring about justice for his chosen ones, who cry out to him day and night? Will he keep putting them off? ⁸ I tell you, he will see that they get justice, and quickly*

Whoever you are, whatever is your situation, Jesus will not reject you. Your solution is nearer than you can imagine. Keep on forging ahead.

The Judge did not frustrate the widow.

Though the judge delayed to answer this widow he did not frustrate her. Though the judge answered this widow because he did not want the woman to weary him, he neither wearied the woman or wear her out. Frustration[10] is a feeling of disappointment and discomfort aroused in the mind of human beings only when something has gone wrong with them or they are not able to achieve the goals that they had set for themselves. In every ten people seven are affected by it and out of them three are severely affected. It is a mental feeling that is growing like other dangerous diseases such as AIDS. It was frustration that drove this woman to the judge. Frustration comes as a result of overwhelming pressures of life. The extent to which the adversary has tormented this woman is not known, however for this woman to go and meet this wicked man means the frustration has become desperation. In the seventies and eighties Christianity was not as popular as it is today. Christians also at that time had a narrow view of their godly inheritance. Many believed then that it was only people who were frustrated who became Christians. The argument then was that something needed to drive you to Jesus. There is nothing wrong if your challenges draw you nearer to the Judge of the universe the Lord Jesus Christ. The judge in this parable realised that this widow was totally frustrated hence he refused to let her go away. Jesus knows our pains. He says "come to me all you that labour and are heavy laden I will give you rest." One of the lessons the judge taught is that no matter how frustrated you are and no matter the delay you are experiencing when you bring those challenges to Jesus, wait on him. He will surely not add to your sorrows. The unfortunate thing however today is that we compound our frustration because we cannot persist. We were not told how long this woman waited but she waited and persisted until she got justice from a wicked judge. Ask yourself how many churches you have attended in one year? In the past 5 years? In the past ten years and more? What is driving you from one church to the other? Has God changed? Why not look beyond the wicked judge who does not fear God and look to the good God whom you have come to meet in that church. The widow could have run out and be on the street joining others to complain about how wicked the judge was. She persisted. Stop complaining about Pastors, General Overseers, Bishops and the like. Bypass them while still remaining in that church and focus on the Judge of the universe. This widow unlike some of us didn't come to try this judge. She did not come to correct him. She came with her frustration, she persisted and got justice.

The Widow

The second character in the parable was a widow. In this parable, the judge and the widow have become the two sides of a coin. We have looked at the side of the judge let us look briefly at what we can glean from the widows' attitude. A widow literally means a person who has lost her husband and has not remarried. She lost a life companion, probably a bread winner and life partner. The Bible has many stories about widows that we can learn from, let us look at one who had a major crisis like the one in this parable.

"The wife of a man from the company of the prophets cried out to Elisha, "Your servant my husband is dead, and you know that he revered the LORD. But now his creditor is coming to take my two boys as his slaves[11]. Widows are most of the time in want, disarrayed and vulnerable as this woman was. Widows need help.

47

The parable shows that even though the society knows about the vulnerability of the widow and you would think they will have a quick response to life issues that concern them it does not happen. Life, whether for a widow or widower is not a drive through. Life is not microwaveable. Life happens. It is slow, full of ups and downs. You go through the rigor, the process of vision. Even if the 'judge' in your case is the most caring and understanding, there are still life issues to contend with. That life issue is what puts a demand on all of us to be persistent.

Listen to what Jesus said is done to widows: *Woe unto you, scribes and Pharisees, hypocrites! for ye devour widows' houses, and for a pretense make long prayer: therefore ye shall receive the greater damnation*[4] (Matthew 23:14)"

Luke the physician is giving us a picture which is told by Jesus about two categories of people, the ruler and the ruled. Jesus is telling us how to approach life from both angles even though he is using a secular set up and analogy he is surely laying a profound foundation as *Master builder* for human interaction, decision making process and relationships. From the widow's perspective that represents the ruled; Jesus was saying persistence is about discipline. Discipline is about vision. Vision is about life goals or accumulation of a series of life goals. Life goals are about life assignments and life assignments are about your purpose.

Let us look critically and closely at the widow

She is a woman.

Jesus chose a widowed woman not a widower to drive his point. Jesus as a master communicator deliberately chose a woman. Bear in mind what the woman's goal was "to avenge me of my adversary."

And there was a widow in that town who kept coming to him with the plea, 'Grant me justice against my adversary NIV

And there was a widow in that city who kept coming to him and saying, Protect and defend and give me justice against my adversary AMP

Diverse as the Bible is with sixty-six books we only see one woman who is Deborah the wife of Lambeth leading war in the book of judges. The rest of the times, women were seen as help mates who needed assistance themselves. Paul was talking about them and says they are 'weaker vessels'

As a widow she is vulnerable to attack. She was looking for Justice. We were not told about the nature of her adversary but going by the society we are today so many things could be deduced. Some people might have been abusing her physically. It could have been the in-laws as is commonly done in some African nations had driven her out of the husband's house that she jointly laboured to build when he was alive. They could have confiscated her husband's company. They could have refused to execute her husband's will as expected. Who knows if they also took away her properties, liquid cash, houses, cars and even children? It was obvious that this woman had an adversary that a widower may not have had and all her efforts were not getting anywhere. So as a widowed woman she reflects a person or society that this society generally treated badly. We also saw her desperation. May be this was why Jesus chose a woman. Women seem to have more stamina and have capacity for persistence. There are many women in the Bible who could be used to buttress the issue of persistence but let us look at four of them,

1.*Delilah* : *With such nagging she prodded him day after day until he was sick to death of it.* Judges 16:16. This woman though on an evil agenda came to Samson the Judge of Israel at that time. She was a spy for her people the Philistines. She employed many tactics to know the strength of Samson. Who wants to easily give away the secret of his source of life and power? surely no one, not Samson. Nevertheless, this woman persisted, pressurised and persuaded Samson until she got what she wanted. The issue here is not to encourage prostitution, or attempt to ruin someone's ministry but to look at the dexterity and temerity by which Delilah approached the Judge of Israel and got what she wanted. You too as a woman or man can come to the Judge of the universe and get results.

2.The Widow's Olive Oil

[1] *The wife of a man from the company of the prophets cried out to Elisha, "Your servant my husband is dead,*

and you know that he revered the LORD. But now his creditor is coming to take my two boys as his slaves."
² Elisha replied to her, "How can I help you? Tell me, what do you have in your house?" "Your servant has nothing there at all," she said, "except a small jar of olive oil." ³ Elisha said, "Go around and ask all your neighbors for empty jars. Don't ask for just a few. ⁴ Then go inside and shut the door behind you and your sons. Pour oil into all the jars, and as each is filled, put it to one side

We can learn from this widow the expected attitude in persistence. She like the widow in the parable under discussion had a great need. Her adversary wanted her to pay the debt she had owed him otherwise the sons will be taken away. She ran to the man of God. "How can I help you" Elisha said. "What do you have in your house?" In the process of persistence we think it is just waiting and doing nothing and expecting miracle. The level of your involvement and investment will determine the result you will get. Some people want to be debt free like this woman. God says, invest your tithe, sow your tithe, the level you are able to sow, the level of financial breakthrough you will have. Rather than obey as this woman did we blame the Pastor who is acting in the capacity of Elisha. Borrow ideas, invest ideas and trust God for the rest

3. The Syrophenician

The woman was a Greek, born in Syrian Phoenicia. She begged Jesus to drive the demon out of her daughter. ²⁷

"First let the children eat all they want," he told her, "for it is not right to take the children's bread and toss it to the dogs." ²⁸ "Lord," she replied, "even the dogs under the table eat the children's crumbs." ²⁹ Then he told her, "For such a reply, you may go; the demon has left your daughter. ³⁰ She went home and found her child lying on the bed, and the demon gone.

We were not told whether this woman was a widow or not but the story made it clear she was not of the stock of Israel. She was not to benefit from the children's bread. However, she had wisdom and humility. Do you quickly get angry over every situation? How do you react to words of provocation from unexpected quarters? This woman wanted her daughter healed. That was her goal, her target and greatest desire. She had heard about Jesus the miracle working man. She had also not heard about Jesus failing to grant anyone's request. She went with a mind that it will be an easy case. She was shocked about Jesus reaction, but she did not show it, rather she absorbed the entire situation in a grand style. That is my recommendation for you.

Esther

Then Esther sent this reply to Mordecai: ¹⁶ "Go, gather together all the Jews who are in Susa, and fast for me. Do not eat or drink for three days, night or day. I and my attendants will fast as you do. When this is done, I will go to the king, even though it is against the law. And if I perish, I perish Esther 4:16

Esther's story showed us as women we can influence issues if we so desire. Esther taught us that we do not just approach the judge casually but with prayers and fasting. Esther taught us determination in approaching the issues of our lives. Esther is not finished, she taught us to that to gain the world for Christ you must be willing to lay down your life. Esther taught us that many at times we need to be interested in the affairs of our community and not just limit our resources to helping only ourselves and immediate family alone. She became a champion for the liberation of the Jews. She employed tact not tactics, wisdom not manipulation, courage not cowardice in the process of national pursuit.

Jesus chose a woman in this parable to show us their strengths, their capabilities, their abilities, their capacity, their discipline to withstand stress, discouragement and get results if they choose to. Reader you have all it takes to make your life better. The judge is there to stretch you but when you stretch your virtue you will smile as these women smiled at the end of their cases.

The widow was defenseless

There are several ways, too, in which the importunate woman could be regarded as defenseless. This woman had **no federal ties**-she had no lawyer who knew the judge to intervene with him on her behalf. She had **no family ties**, was not related to the judge by birth or adoption. She had **no friendship ties**; if she had they must have let her down very badly. She probably would have heard about how stern, uncaring or heartless this judge could be. Nevertheless, the lack of friends drove her to desperation. She had **no fiscal ties**; no money to pay her debtors and none to use as a bribe. *For wisdom is a **defence**, and money is a **defence**: but the excellency of knowledge is, that wisdom giveth life to them that have i*t Eccl 7:14. She probably had no **religious ties, she might have gone to** see a pastor. She might have believed that going to church was a waste of time just like some of the atheists, revolutionists or agnostics of our time who spend the time to say there is no God. She might have been the freelance Christian who cannot sit in one church and be involved in the activities. Finally, she had **no future ties**. Upon granting her request, he had no further interest in her or any future needs she might have expressed.

The widow was poor

This woman had no money to pay a lawyer hence she had to come and face the ordeal of a stern if not a wicked judge. She sure deserved commendation for a courageous and bold step. If the reason for her being tormented was the widow's inability to pay her creditors and this led the way to her children being taken to slavery then the widow must have suffered abject poverty. She might have been too principled to give bribe but even if she was not; the widow in question surely did not have the means. Poverty is a disease. Poverty is a curse. Poverty has led many to do ridiculous things. I read the story on the Internet about what happened in one of the African nations. A couple was very poor. The woman was enduring the poverty. Then one day the wife's father died. She had to bury her father, so she summoned up courage and asked the husband to give her money to go and bury her dad. "I have endured enough, I am the first born of my late dad give me money to give my dad a decent burial ". The husband did not reply but left the presence of his wife. The third day his corpse was seen dangling on a tree in the early morning. He left a note for the wife. "I have decided to take my life. I have no money to take care of my wife and children and not even money to bury the dead who is my father in law"

There was another story I hope things have changed in that African nation where many of their young girls started trooping to Italy for prostitution. It became such a menace that the government decided to work with the Italian counterpart to repatriate them. When they were eventually brought back to their country of origin, the media interviewed some of them. The reason some of them gave was that they were poor. Poverty has driven people to assassination, armed robbery, embezzlement of public fund, kidnapping and all manner of crimes. The crimes have even metamorphosed from what could be called 'traditional crimes' to modern or computer aided ones. All manner of fraudulent practices all bordering on money laundering. These and many others are what people are driven to do in the name of poverty. The widow will not do any of these she wanted a legitimate life style. Poverty did not take away her common sense. Poverty did not make her a nuisance to the society. She was pursuing restoration through due process. She was pursuing justice without hiring a lawyer or legal aid. She knew what she was up to. She realised that the judge was still a human being subject to reasons. She knew that if she was willing to pay the price of persistence she would get a good result. She realised her weapon was importunity, determination, ruggedness and faithfulness. Jesus told us that she strategically approached the issues of her life. Jesus wanted us to have a strategy for overcoming issues of life even when we do not have obvious means to accomplish great things. Jesus taught us through the poverty of this woman that you and I can overcome poverty. I like the way John Maxwell put it. When you are at a cross road you have two options, you either give up or you ask for help. This woman did not give up she asked for help.

The widow saw the judge as the last hope

Sometimes we serve God out of ignorance and it does not help us to know or see what or who God is. There is no alternative to our God. The judge was the only hope for this widow, so she could not afford to lose heart. Jesus is your only hope. Satan cannot be an alternative to Jesus. Hell cannot be an alternative to heaven. You know what you need to do. You do not compare death and sleep. This woman was not bothered if this man was of the same faith or not she just knew this was her only hope and so she was not going anywhere. God can use anyone to bless us whether it is a believer or unbeliever. The Israelites were freed from captivity by a gentile king. When you know there is no alternative to Jesus no matter how long your waiting period is you will persist. Unfortunately today many pastors cannot wait like Esther in prayer and fasting they now result to engaging herbalists, psychics to get crowds to church. It is the name of Jesus that can cause your church to grow and you will still make heaven. It is the name of Jesus that can help your business to grow. This widow was willing to wait, can you wait on the Lord? *But they that wait upon the LORD shall renew their strength; they shall mount up with wings as eagles; they shall run, and not be weary; and they shall walk, and not faint. Isaiah 40:31*

CHAPTER FOUR

THE ART OF PERSISTENCE

The major focus of this book is to teach how to persevere in the journey of life, that is why John Maxwell said "wisdom is knowing what to do next, skill is knowing how to do it and virtue is doing it." If you have read up to this point you have shown interest in perseverance and demonstrated you can persevere and so I congratulate you. Some people find it difficult to be persistent in small things and they want to be persistent in big things, it does not work like that. Though there are many lessons from this parable, some of the underlying principles God is making clear is that we shall face challenges on earth; like the widow. The question we are facing is; when things appear to be at their lowest ebb, how can you still make the best out of it? Where do we find the inspiration to keep going when it seems that everything around us is falling apart? How do we find the desire to succeed when the odds seem insurmountable? How do we react when trouble finds us and singles us out? How do we react when our spouse walks out on us? How do you react when you read a line on your e-mail from your employer early in the morning "We forgot to mention it at the close of work yesterday, we appreciate your services in this company, however due to circumstances beyond our control your services will no more be required with immediate effect." What do you do when there is a text message "We are sorry to inform you but so and so died 3pm yesterday EST." What do you do with your life when the phone rings "Is that Mr. XYZ?, I am calling from the Police homicide Division, There was a shootout at your neighborhood around noon and unfortunately Mr. ABC was one of the victims shot, we understand he is your relation; he is at the ICU at Homerton Hospital?" Is that the end of your life? Is there no way out? Jesus teaches in this parable there is a way out. No matter what you are going through there is hope in knowing that God is still in control. There is a judge who may not respond quickly but if you will persist he will give you satisfactory justice. This chapter will help you to learn how to be persistent. Fasten your seat belts.

Walk in the spirit of God's revelation

The vehicle for God's revelation and creation is words, his words. To ignore the words of God is to revel in your perils. It is not in vain or for fun that the scripture started creation by allowing the Spirit of God to survey the earth, notice not just on the surface but moved over the deep of the waters, that shows the survey was in-depth[1]. The more you allow the understanding of the word coupled with the walking in the guidance of the spirit the more you are able to face the issues of life and be able to persist. Let me start by helping you with three characters that span three generations; how they went on the same journey and how God gave them different instructions. When God called Abraham he gave him a lot of promises. I guess when you became a Christian you were exposed to eight thousand promises in the Bible. Sounds familiar?

[1]NOW [in Haran] the Lord said to Abram, Go for yourself [for your own advantage] away from your country, from your relatives and your father's house, to the land that I will show you. [2]And I will make of you a great nation, and I will bless you [with abundant increase of favors] and make your name famous and distinguished, and you will be a blessing [dispensing good to others]. [3]And I will bless those who bless you [who confer prosperity or happiness upon you] and curse him who curses or uses insolent language toward you; in you will all the families and kindred of the earth be blessed [and by you they will bless themselves]. [4]So Abram departed, as the Lord had directed him; and Lot [his nephew] went with him. Abram was seventy-five years old when he left Haran. [5]Abram took Sarai his wife, and Lot his brother's son, and all their possessions that they had gathered, and the persons [servants] that they had acquired in Haran, and they went forth to go to the land of Canaan. When they came to the land of Canaan, [6]Abram passed through the land to the locality of Shechem, to the oak or terebinth tree of Moreh. And the Canaanite was then in the land. [7]Then

*the Lord appeared to Abram and said, I will give this
land to your posterity. So Abram built an altar there
to the Lord, Who had appeared to him. ⁸From there he
pulled up [his tent pegs] and departed to the mountain
on the east of Bethel and pitched his tent, with Bethel
on the west and Ai on the east; and there he built an
altar to the Lord and called upon the name of the Lord.
⁹Abram journeyed on, still going toward the South (the
Negeb). ¹⁰Now there was a famine in the land, and
Abram ⁽ᵇ⁾went down into Egypt to live temporarily,
for the famine in the land was oppressive (intense and
grievous).*

The scripture says in verse four he departed. In verse 8 he
started enjoying fellowship with God. He built an altar
in Bethel. He proceeded on the journey. In verse ten, he
encountered famine. The comparison I am interested
in is how Abraham, Isaac and Jacob faced famine in
three generations. Now I am not going to tell you too
much about famine but give you some synonyms: food
shortage, scarcity, starvation, food crisis, dearth, want
and deprivation. What did Abraham do? He fled. He
fled to Egypt. It boomeranged on him. In Egypt he
started to mess up. He lost his dignity. He relegated
his wife status to sister level. He stopped telling the
complete truth to half—truth. He feared for his life
at the expense of that of his wife who was his most
precious possession. He walked in the flesh. Reason?
Though he had the promises he could not imagine how
with such promises famine could be included in the
package. Later he found out barrenness was part of the
package. I am always amazed when out of the eight
thousand promises in the Bible all we claim are the

positive and most comfortable ones. In John 14:27 the scripture says "in this world we shall have trouble!" I wonder how many of us claim such promises, but whether we do or not we face troubles in this world

Let us look at his son, Isaac. In Genesis chapter twenty-six he faced the same monstrous famine. He wanted to get out of Gerar and run to Egypt but he had a check in his spirit. This time he walked in the spirit. He listened to God. God said "do not go to Egypt." The scripture says he did not only prosper he waxed great in Gerar. So much striving, so much blocking of the well but because he was told this is where he would make it he walked in the spirit of the revelation. He became the envy of his generation. Was there no more famine? There was still famine but walking in the spirit, listening and obeying God in the situation helped him out. When you are faced with challenges find out what God's word has to say about them.

Let's look at Abraham's grandson, the son of Isaac, his name has been changed from Jacob to Israel. He was faced with that monster again called famine. This time the famine was of a greater proportion. It was no more a local problem it was a global recession. The only place food was available was Egypt. Egypt again? He probably had heard how Abraham went and it did not do him much good. How Isaac wanted to go and God said no. Jacob feared going to Egypt. God had to beg him to go!

And God spoke to Israel in visions of the night, and said, Jacob! Jacob! And he said, Here am I. ³And

He said, I am God, the God of your father; do not be afraid to go down to Egypt, for I will there make of you a great nation Gen 46:2-3

The way to be persistent is to grab the word of God and get a revelation of the word of God and walk in the spirit of that revelation. You must hear God yourself. The fact that your parents went through a difficult life does not mean that will be your portion. The fact that your friend or Christian brothers are handling a situation in a particular way does not mean that is the way you will do it. God gave three people in three different generations' different ways of handling the same problem.

Do not walk in the flesh

This I say then, Walk in the Spirit, and ye shall not fulfil the lust of the flesh. [17]For the flesh lusteth against the Spirit, and the Spirit against the flesh: and these are contrary the one to the other: so that ye cannot do the things that ye would Gal 5:16-17

So that you will not fulfill the lust of the flesh. The flesh lusted to envy. The flesh is impatient. The flesh will make you to giraffe and try and look at what God is doing in one person's life and compare it to yours. Most times that approach will give you an impression that person's life is better than yours and you will be tempted to eliminate your life forgetting to realize that everyone has a problem even if it is not visible to others. The flesh will not make you to see how beautiful or wonderful you are, all the flesh will show you is how bad God is for allowing some tiny pimples on your face for a season. The flesh will not allow you to see how many exams you have passed in life but will continually remind you of the Summer school you will be going because you failed a course out of ten in Spring. Listen to me; in order to be persistent is to realise that the Spirit is superior to the flesh. This is because the flesh is limited and the spirit is unlimited. The flesh will die but the spirit lives on forever and ever. Always remember man is a spirit he has a soul and lives in a body. The morning of the day I was writing this portion of the book I went to the funeral of a 30 year old young man. The flesh was glittering; courtesy of the Funeral Home—during the viewing a well decorated coffin was surrounded with beautiful flowers; it was as if the young man was sleeping. I cried like a baby, alongside the father who is a pastor. That is all we could do. His spirit was gone. He was a young man who knew the Lord. Soon that flesh will decay but the Spirit will glitter forever. The flesh is earthly. It came from the earth and to earth it will always return. At the burial site the funeral words were recited to all by all of us—dust to dust, ashes to ashes and earth to earth!

Walk in the newness of your of life.

Do not frustrate the grace of God in your life. Salvation is by grace through faith not of works. Jesus has set you free. Jesus has paid a price for you. Salvation is a gift, but salvation was not cheap for Jesus. Grace cost

Jesus his life at the prime age of thirty-three. Jesus said *it is finished*. Not that he is finished because he is not finished he lives forever more. All you need to help you go through life has been accomplished for you. The reason we are so easily and quickly discouraged is because we fail to appropriate the great work our Master did for us. Many times we are struggling to achieve what he has done for us. We are walking in self-condemnation, working in self-righteousness and working in self-holiness. The energy we needed to do exploits is channelled at doing what he has already done. Righteousness is a gift.

For if, by the trespass of the one man, death reigned through that one man, how much more will those who receive God's abundant provision of grace and of the gift of righteousness reign in life through the one man, Jesus Christ. Romans 5:17

Sin and its consequences came through Adam because he walked in the flesh. Jesus walked in the Spirit and was able to conquer Satan and wriggle us from the power of sin. When Jesus was tempted to turn stone to bread he refused, when tempted to jump he refused, when tempted to worship Satan he refused. He walked in the spirit. There was no short cut. If he had fasted for 40 days and forty nights he could as well have gotten home to break his fast rather than approving a suggested short cut from Satan. When as a young girl you cannot wait for a proper marriage but you are engaging yourself in fornication and adultery with the married ones just to have some money or gratification you are turning stone to bread. Wait.

Walk in the revelation of God's word.

You are a new creature old things have passed away. The Spirit of God dwells in you from the day you gave your life to Christ. This means that Christ has enabled you; do not disable yourself. The day Joseph was called out of prison he changed his cloth. Change your garment. Have you seen the movie stars? Once they attain the celebrity status they change their dress code. Change your dress spiritually and physically. Look at the person God has made you to become. If you are a relief worker and you are promoted to the position of a Managing Director or Chief Executive Officer of a well established business organization your dressing will change! Friend your case is more, Jesus said you were a 'slave' but you are now promoted to a 'friend.' Paul said you were a 'slave' but you are now joint heirs with Jesus. Celebrate!

Walk by faith

One day a six-year-old girl was sitting in a classroom. The teacher was going to explain evolution to the children. The teacher asked the little boy:

Teacher: "Tommy do you see the tree outside?"

Tommy: "Yes."

Teacher: "Tommy, do you see the grass outside?"
Tommy: "Yes."

Teacher: "Go outside and look up, and see if you can see the sky."

Tommy: "Okay." (He returned a few minutes later) "Yes, I saw the Sky."

Teacher: "Did you see God?"

Tommy: "No."

Teacher: "That's my point. We can't see God because He isn't there, he doesn't exist."

A little girl spoke up and wanted to ask the boy some questions. The teacher agreed and the little girl asked the boy:

Little Girl: "Tommy, do you see the tree outside?"

Tommy: "Yes."

: Little Girl "Tommy, do you see the grass outside?"

Tommy: "Yessssss (getting tired of the same questions by this time)."

Little Girl: "Did you see the sky?"

Tommy: "Yessssss."

Little Girl: "Do you see the teacher?"

Tommy: "Yes."

Little Girl: "Do you see her brain?"

Tommy: "No."

Little Girl: "Then according to what we were taught today in school, she must not have one!"

> *"For we walk by faith not by sight."*
> 2 Corinthians 5:7

I believe this story is the best way to explain faith. Many people claim to believe in God, but do they really have faith in Him? You see it is not a big deal to believe that there is a God and that Jesus exists. Even Satan knows that. The true test of our faith is—do we trust Him? Are we willing to put our hand in the hand of the man that stilled the water? Are we willing to go where He asks us to go and do what He asks us to do? Do we trust Him with our finances? Do we trust Him in our relationships? Do we trust Him in our everyday walk and in the choices we make in life? I recently saw a film where a pastor asked every man in the room to stand up, and take out his wallet. Then he was asked to exchange wallets with the guy standing next to him. Then he was asked to reach into that wallet and give the way he always wanted to give! Of course it was a joke and the pastor told everyone to hand the wallet back to the rightful owner, but the point was made, that when we give someone else's money, it's easy; but when we give our own money, it's hard. The believer needs to realize that everything he has comes from God, and it belongs to God anyway. That is true faith.

What distinguished Abraham as a man of faith? He was willing to give a son he had waited for, for over twenty-five. Abraham must have been one hundred years old when he had Isaac. The boy was probably twelve years old during the period of the sacrifice thereby making Abraham one hundred and twelve years old but he was still willing to give away his son. The son asked 'a great question' in Genesis verse seven 'My father where is the lamb for the offering?' Abraham gave a 'greater answer' in verse eight. 'My God will provide a lamb for the offering' we give up in life because we cannot see God making that provision. We refuse to be faithful in life because the money in our hands is not enough to pay our bills. You walk out of that marriage because you are simply impatient. You walk out of that school because you cannot persist. There is nothing wrong with that business, what you are going through is gestation and a break-even period is ahead. There is nothing wrong with the Canaan land or even with the giants. Did God not know there were giants? The Israelites were myopic. They need not have been. They had seen God display His power in Egypt, in the parting of the Red Sea, in the supernatural supply of manna. Instead of seeing with the eyes of faith they saw with the eyes of discouragement. Yet, they concluded they could not see the land and they perished in the wilderness Sometimes we make decisions based on how we see the situation. It is God who knows the end from the beginning. We live by faith not by sight. Ecc 7:8. My friend you don't have to turn the journey of forty days to forty years due to lack of faith and failure to persist. The giants in Jericho died when people were playing music and dancing around the walls. Many of you today will not even get to service until praise and worship is over. You are always excited when it is time to bind the devil but the giants kill themselves during praise and worship, for God inhabits the praise of men. God comes down when we are praising him and stays up when we are praying to him.

Go through the trials.

Have you heard people say—"go through, grow in it and you will glow." What they are referring to is trails most of the time. If you want the anointing of God, you are going to go through trials. If you want financial blessings, you are going to through trials. If you want a family, you are going to go through trials, whatever you want—God is going to allow you to go through trials. God never said there will be no river that has the capacity to drown you. God never promised that there will be no fire which can burn you to ashes. He gave you one promise which is—I will be with you. When Samson totally messed up and was going through trials, his two eyes were plugged out; his hair the source of his power was shaved. He was grinding pepper for his enemies. However, he had a life assignment to destroy the enemies of God. Therefore, God saw to it that his hair grew back again. He held the pillars of that hall and killed more people in death even in his disability than when he was able bodied. The three Hebrew men were thrown in the fire. God has power to make sure they did not get into that fire. Nevertheless, he preferred to show up as the fourth person in the fire. God has power to prevent Daniel from entering the

Lion's den, but he had to go through it. Your trial is a stepping stone to your success. You will not stop going through trials till you die, it will just be at different levels and to bring different success. The earlier you learn to persist in trials and learn how to handle it in a better way rather than praying against it the better. He prepared a table before me in the presence of my enemies. Jesus went through his own trials till he died, thank God he resurrected. Did Joseph not go through trials?

Delay is not denial

Delay is not denial; a knock down is not a knock out. Lazarus was sick, a very good friend of Jesus. Mary and Martha sent for Jesus but he deliberately tarried. It was as if he was making jest of the situation. The Bible said he failed to show up when Lazarus was sick and when he eventually died they sent a message to him that he was dead. Jesus told his disciples Lazarus is sleeping! The disciples said—that is not a problem we shall go and wake him up. He said you don't understand, Lazarus is dead, but relax Jesus raised dead Lazarus after four days. Delay is not denial. Your dead womb is not a problem. It will come alive. Many women had delayed conception in the Bible but they all gave birth to bouncing baby boys at the appropriate time. Those who could not wait like Sarah knew what she suffered. You remember how she begged her husband to go to her maid, Hagar and Abraham jumped at the opportunity. When Hagar continued to tease and mock her she learnt her lesson. She did not only drive her away but the Bible said she 'received strength to conceive because she thought him faithful who has promised[3].'' The problem of her failure to *wait patiently* caused the whole world a major problem, which is still unresolved today—The Israel—Arab nations conflict.

A pastor told me how he was working with a big government organization. The company wanted to send people abroad for training to run their plant. This young pastor wanted to travel also. However, God showed him in a dream the list of those to travel and his name was not among. He argued with God "Dear God all these people going are not born again Christians, I am a born again Christian, why will you not allow me to go" God was silent. Meanwhile this young Pastor was planting a church that was just six months old and the trip he was agitating to make was for six months. The only visible assistant he had in the church was travelling abroad compulsorily for three years courtesy of his own company. God had a plan for this pastor and he deliberately delayed his traveling abroad as he personally narrated later which he did not know. At the end of the day he did not travel and he concentrated on building the church. He kept praying to God and telling God that he was being owed a trip abroad. After ten years, God opened the doors for him. Only God knows how many nations he has traveled to in the cause of ministering and preaching the gospel of Jesus Christ. As a matter of fact, he now lives abroad. Many people quit because they do not like to wait. You need to learn that delay is not denial. God is never late. God does not count time the way we count time. A thousand years to God is like a day and a day is like a thousand years. David waited many years to become the King of the entire nation of Israel. He faced a lot of battles, but he waited for his time. Your time of glorious victory will come. Joseph had a dream at the age of seventeen he became the prime minister using our modern day political terminology at the age of thirty years, not in Israel but in a land where he was an immigrant. That thing you are waiting for will come. Have you heard 'slow and steady wins the race?' 'Why not fast and steady' I used to ask as a younger Christian? The delay you are experiencing is teaching you how to walk with God. There are many things we could learn from Elijah, one of them is that delay is not denial. He knew how to persist in prayer. He was told by the widowed woman that her son was dead He prayed three times stretching himself on the dead child. He was not praying in unbelief, just hoping he was praying expecting. (I King 17). Look at the final stage of the Mt Carmel encounter with the prophets of Baal and Ahab. He prayed for three years that rain will stop as a result of judgment. Now it was time again to restore rain because judgment had been rendered. When Elijah went to pray he was watching and waiting for God to answer,(is that our attitude today?) he called out seven times before there was slightest indication that rain was coming. Six times he heard, 'There is nothing' Yet he never quit praying. He prayed once and rain stopped and had to pray seven times for rain to be restored. He knew delay was not going to be a denial. James says Elijah was a man like us, the question is, are we men or women like Elijah? (I King 18:41-46, James 5:17-18)

The Power of the Holy Ghost

In my former church the Christ Apostolic Church one of the things I enjoyed is their emphasis on the power of the Holy Ghost. Maybe that is why they call it "Apostolic Church." In my Christian journey I see a lot of people arguing over many doctrines. In defense of them and trying not to be controversial I will not want to join them in that debate, but for Christians to argue about the power of the Holy Ghost is very strange. What distinguishes a believer from an unbeliever if not for the presence of the Holy Ghost in the life of a person? To me the air the Christians breathe is the Holy Ghost. Take away the power of the Holy Ghost in the life of a Christian and he will totally collapse because there is no more oxygen! A powerless Christian is not a Christian at all, Paul declares[4]. It makes sense when you look at the life of Peter. Peter, a physically bold and overtly outspoken personality was seen in the four synoptic gospels as rising today and falling tomorrow. He was hot today and cold the next day. He was always speaking the words that made Jesus commend him this hour but he got the rebuke of the Master the next minute. He can be best described as consistently inconsistent. He got to the anticlimax when he denied Jesus Christ three times based on weather issues and most likely issues to save his life during the most crucial time that Jesus needed him. But the same Peter joined the one hundred and twenty faithful brethren at the upper room, when he was totally baptized and saturated by the power of the Holy Ghost, the story of his life was changed for good. Peter became a fiery preacher, a miracle worker and an outstanding leader.

In Acts chapter five aware of the raw power of the Holy Ghost in him, he simply confronted Ananias and Saphira for lying to the Holy Ghost. That was not just the end of service that day for the lying couple but the end of their sojourn on earth. You need to be baptized in the Holy Ghost otherwise just asking you to pray will just be enacting a law in a statue book without provision for enforcement. It is the power of the Holy Ghost coupled with the gift of speaking in tongues that makes a Christian to pray through. Telling you to be persistent when facing life challenges without you being baptized in the Holy Ghost is like asking you to climb Mount Kilimanjaro with a one thousand pound luggage on your back! It is practically impossible. A Christian without the Holy Ghost is like the car without an engine. He is fanciful on the outside based on the latest model but incapable of functioning. If you really want to pray through in your life and persevere with ease in any of your endeavors you will need to daily refill your life's tank with the fresh power of the Holy Ghost. No wonder, The Psalmist said "My *horn shall be lifted up like a unicorn and I shall be anointed with fresh oil*" meaning your elevation, your daily promotion is based on your daily provision of fresh anointing.

Faith without Works is Dead

James argues faith is good but it cannot stand alone, and it has to be supported with works. This was the propelling force that moved that widowed woman to action. I guess she could have been praying about her adversary alone, but she understood that faith without works is dead. She added works to her faith and then went to the judge, believing that through this judge God will handle her case. Seventy disciples had just returned from a preaching assignment and were reporting their experiences to the Lord[7]. Overjoyed, Jesus said, "I praise you, O Father, Lord of heaven and earth, that you have hidden these things from the wise and intelligent and have revealed them to infants." Turning to his disciples, he said "Blessed are the eyes which see the things you see." In the midst of this joyful revelry, a lawyer, an expert in the Law of Moses, stands up to test Jesus:

"Teacher, what shall I do to inherit eternal life?" Moreover, he said to him, "What is written in the Law? How does it read to you?" And he answered, "You shall love the Lord your God with all your heart, and with all your soul, and with all your strength, and with your entire mind; and your neighbor as yourself." And he said to him, "You have answered correctly; do this and you will live." But wishing to justify himself, he said to Jesus, "And who is my neighbor[8]? Jesus answered with the parable of the Good Samaritan. *A man was attacked by robbers while traveling from Jerusalem to Jericho. A priest and a Levite both pass by, offering no help, leaving him to die. However, a Samaritan stops and helps the man at considerable time and expense, bandaging his wounds and carrying him to an inn. "Which of these three do you think proved to be a neighbor to the man who fell into the robbers' hands?" And he said, "The one who showed mercy toward him." Then Jesus said to him, "Go and do the same."*

The lawyer had asked, "Who is my neighbor?" The Greek word is *pleesion* which can mean any other person, or it can mean a friend. The lawyer wanted to know to whom he should direct his love. In effect, Jesus tells him that the question should not be "who is my neighbor" but rather "how can I be a friend to those who are in need." The answer is simple: provide help irrespective of race or background. Pursue your goal with both practical and spiritual fervor. It is unfortunate to say many Christians are lazy. They spiritualize everything and ignore the practical aspect.

Jesus is teaching that actions speak louder than appearances. The priest and Levite, who appeared righteous and God-fearing, revealed their hypocrisy through their inaction. Only the Samaritan, an outcast from Jewish society, acted as the real neighbor.

We know that works in themselves cannot save anyone[9] However, good works naturally follow if there is faith in the heart. "You have faith and I have works; show me your faith without the works, and I will show you my faith by my works[10]." Good works prove that we are "sons of [our] Father who is in heaven; for he causes his sun to rise on the evil and the good, and sends rain on the righteous and the unrighteous[11]"

The Good Samaritan story also teaches us persistence. Why will the Priest and the Levite not wait? They were in a hurry among many other things. They would not have wanted to miss their appointments probably. They obviously do not know love hence they could not persist in it. On the other hand, the good Samaritan had the love of the neighbor and persisted in it at the risk of his life he waited and took care of the armed robbers' fallen victim.

To further buttress our point on what to learn from the parable we shall use the acronym of persistence.

The Acronym of P.E.R.S.I.S.T.E.N.C.E

P—Put all the resources in gear. Your life is worth whatever it will cost you. Time, energy, talent, treasure, prayer, virtue, patience, importunity, meekness, brotherly kindness, to pursue your passion and God given dream and never quit if you genuinely want a breakthrough in life. There is a price for success. Pour your life into your vision. Life will want to wear you out refuse to be worn out. Life will want to mess you up refuse to be messed up.

E. Exercise wisdom. The scripture says wisdom is the principal thing, get wisdom and not worldly wisdom of short cuts, bribery and compromise but of patience and long suffering when necessity calls for it. Solomon knew that he needed wisdom to manage a throne that by *right* will never have been his but by the grace *of* God in his life. He was presiding over a divided family. He needed wisdom to rule the nation of Israel. You need wisdom to manage your family. You need wisdom to handle your unbeliever spouse. Friend, you need wisdom to keep yourself a virgin and wait for the right man to marry you. You never can tell you may be the Ester to replace Vashti but if you cannot allow wisdom to help you wait patiently you may never become a queen that God has destined you to become. The great book say "*he that hateth to be rich shall has an evil eye, and considereth not that poverty shall come upon him[12].*". *As the partridge sitteth on eggs, and hatcheth them not; so he that getteth* **riches**, *and not by right, shall leave them in the midst of his days, and at his end shall be a fool[13]. But the wisdom that is from above is first pure, then peaceable, gentle, and easy to be intreated, full of mercy and good fruits, without partiality, and without hypocrisy*[14]

Persistence is not just about waiting it is about waiting while exercising wisdom. Every day you take decisions. The decision of yesterday led to where you are today. The decision of where you will be tomorrow is what you are taking today so apply wisdom. Are you building a ministry, business, institution, career, wisdom will help you and me. How do you have wisdom? Pray to God for wisdom. Learn to read books, particularly biographies and autobiographies they are full of real nuggets and life experiences. Move in the company of achievers. When you are with aged people listen to them and deliberately ask questions. Many of them are on their way out and you need to get what they have. It will take wisdom to live and work among people that do not share your values or Christian passion when you meet such people every day. The world system is very corrupt and God is not ready to take you out of the world. You are still needed on this planet but you will face issues like other people. While others will easily bribe their way out you cannot, you need wisdom. The woman who took her case to an unjust judge was exercising wisdom. She knew litigation takes time in any nation. She knew if she did not deal with the man according to wisdom she will just deny herself justice and she will be the loser. We cannot serve God without knowledge and understanding. We will lose out. Big time

Somebody forwarded a write up to me through my email about *winner versus loser*. The summary of it is the loser really uses wisdom enjoy.

Winner Versus Loser

The Winner is always part of the answer;
The Loser is always part of the problem.

The Winner always has a program;
The Loser always has an excuse.

The Winner says, "Let me do it for you";
The Loser says, "That is not my job."

The Winner sees an answer for every problem;
The Loser sees a problem for every answer.

The Winner says, "It may be difficult but it is possible";
The Loser says, "It may be possible but it is too difficult."

When a Winner makes a mistake, he says, "I was wrong";
When a Loser makes a mistake, he says, "It wasn't my fault."

A Winner makes commitments;
A Loser makes promises.

Winners have dreams;
Losers have schemes.

Winners say, "I must do something";
Losers say, "Something must be done."

Winners are a part of the team;
Losers are apart from the team.

Winners see the gain;
Losers see the pain.

Winners see possibilities;
Losers see problems.

Winners believe in win-win;
Losers believe for them to win someone has to lose.

Winners see the potential;
Losers see the past.

Winners are like a thermostat;
Losers are like thermometers.

Winners choose what they say;
Losers say what they choose.

Winners use hard arguments but soft words;
Losers use soft arguments but hard words.

Winners stand firm on values but compromise on petty things;
Losers stand firm on petty things but compromise on values.

Winners follow the philosophy of empathy: "Don't do to others what you would not want them to do to you";
Losers follow the philosophy, "Do it to others before they do it to you."

Winners make it happen;
Losers let it happen.

Winners plan and prepare to win.
The key word is preparation.

R—Refuse to be distracted.

Most denominations in Christendom teach that you close your eyes when praying. This is to help you concentrate. So many laws are enacted in many nations against people driving and texting. Other laws are also against drinking alcohol and driving. If you are driving and you lose your concentration for less than a minute it can cost you your life and jeopardize passengers in your car and terminate the lives of other innocent road users. If just driving a car demands such extra care why don't you think your life journey is too critical for you not to be distracted. The widow did not only stay in the unjust man's house she continued to make her demand. "Avenge me of my adversary" she kept crying. In a similar story in Luke Chapter 11 the man asked for his friend to take care of the needy. Our generation has unfortunately become a prayerless generation because of a major life distraction—the pursuit of dollars. Night vigils in the western world have disappeared. Men have no time to pray any more. No wonder in "*Godfathers never sleep"* By J.K Randle, he made a caricature of this generation. Apparently referring to the incident where Peter healed the lame man after declaring that "silver and gold I do not have but what I have I give to you rise up and walk[15]." He said the Peter of today cannot necessarily say silver and gold I do not have and that is why they cannot also say to a lame man "Rise and walk". Too much game and television viewing has distracted our children from being the best God has made them. Your brain needs to be tasked on a better level to function well. Researchers say human beings use only ten percent of their brain potentials. Stay focused on your life pursuit. Champions are made not born. Champions are people who made up their minds as to where they want to excel and they stay focused till they become. There is nothing wrong if you don't initially know where you are going in life, but once you find your bearing you will regret if you allow anyone, any situation and any circumstance to prevent you. Will you be distracted or find your way back and maintain it? Obama Barack was distracted early in life when he started experimenting with drugs and hanging around gangs. However, the moment he discovered that route was not on the way to the White House but to correction jail he found his way back until he was sworn in as the 44th President of the United States. I watched him campaign for more than 21 months, flying from one state to the other, giving countless speeches. The odds were insurmountable. He was not even a regular Black American but a continental Black American with a father from Kenya. Whatever page you are in your life now try and be focused. May be your church is not growing. Maybe the course you are studying is too tough. Maybe you are even in prison and you think it is over. No. It was your being distracted that got you there, straighten your life there in that situation and discover what you were born to do and refuse to be distracted and you will get there. Avoid distraction, persist and you will get there. Remember the Judge on the throne now is no more the wicked judge. The judge on the throne is a loving God. He encourages us in Matthew chapter seven to ask, seek and knock. He is saying that asking may not produce result, go ahead and seek if that still did not work, engage in the process of knocking. When you do he says your earthly father will not give you different things from what you are asking for. For instance if you ask for bread they will not give you stone, if you ask for an egg they will not give you serpent. So if you ask me I will give you your heart desire promptly. *"Then the Lord said, "Learn a lesson from this unjust judge. [7] Even he rendered a just decision in the end. So don't you think God will surely give justice to his chosen people who cry out to him day and night? Will he keep putting them off? [8] I tell you, he will grant justice to them quick[16] "*

S—Speak positive affirmations about yourself and your situation. The Israelites were so precious to God that he was not willing to destroy any one in the wilderness. But when they got the report of the ten spies who had a bad report they believed it and continue to confess that they were not able to possess the land until God got angry with them. "*This is the tenth time you said you will die in this wilderness, I will therefore ensure your carcasses are wasted here*" declared God. Persistence is not just about continuing with what you are doing, it is about the attitude, motivation and confession by which you are doing it. What is the point for a group of people to be going on a journey but they never believed it was the best for them? God loves us. God cares about us but he wants us to have a positive attitude about Him and ourselves. That is what distinguished Joshua and Caleb. "*If thy Lord delights in us he will give us the land*" declared the duo. My friend God delights in you. He delights in your success. Now that you are a widow God still has a plan for the rest of your life to help you succeed. It is not the plan of God that you will be separated from your spouse or even go through a very bitter divorce. It is not the plan of God that you will become a single parent. It is not the plan of God that you should be raised by foster parents or step parents. Nevertheless, God still loves you as you are. Stop condemning yourself. Stop saying bad things to yourself. Will the righteous God not do better than the wicked judge? The widow understood that God can change the situation through the judge. God will use an uncommon source to give you laughter instead of sorrow. Prophesy to yourself, and your situation "I will make it", "I will not be swallowed up in the wilderness of life.", I break and destroy the circle of failure over my life. I will be successful. Faith is not necessary if the conditions are favourable. Faith is about you believing that God can turn a hopeless situation around no matter the case. "As truly as I live," says thy Lord "whatever you say to my ears I will do?" Your son is rebellious and you keep cursing him, how does that help your life? Your business is not doing well and all you do is murmur, will murmuring help you? Begin to speak life to that dead situation until you see a positive change that is how to persist. The widow did not go to the judge to complain but to make a demand! "Avenge me of my adversary?" Or "Protect me from my adversary." No room for rhetoric. She was drowning. Speak life to your dead situation and see the scenario change for the better. That is how to persist and possess your possession. There is power of life and death in your tongue.

I—Imagine your greatest potential and work to achieve it. Inside an egg is a fowl. When thunder strikes it is usually accompanied by fire. When you tap a piano that is connected to a power source it will produce a sound according to your dexterity. When rain falls, it isn't hot water but cold. A newly born girl of today is the mother of tomorrow. You are endued with talent, power, creativity, innovation, stamina, ability and capability! I like the promotional message of Scotia bank in Canada—You are richer than you think! Potential is not what you have done in the past, but what you are able to do in the future. You can therefore create whatever you desire. In other words, you are the producer, director, and actor of your own life. To illustrate this point, here's an article reported in the French newspaper *Le Matin*: "A man was locked in by error in a cold storage room. Thinking he was a prisoner of the cold, this man instantly felt its deadly effects—he froze up and became paralyzed. During his agony, he managed to find enough strength to write his impressions on the wall with a piece of chalk. When his body was discovered the next morning, it showed all the signs of a man frozen to death. This tragic accident turned out to be extraordinary when it was discovered that the electric generator of the storage room was not out of order, meaning the man shouldn't have died from the cold. Yet, he killed himself . . . by the sheer force of his conviction".

In Matthew chapter twenty five, Jesus gave the parable of the talent. I will like to call it the parable of the potentials. The man who had five potentials traded them with the man who had two thereby reaping a hundred percent each. The man who would easily have got a hundred percent by trading with one talent went and buried it while waiting to blame the master. He succeeded in doing that but lost out on the real issue of life, the failure to make use of his talent. The widow who wasn't taken aback by the nature of the judge created a fortune for herself. Hear the response of the wicked judge:

And for a time he would not; but later he said to himself, Though I have neither reverence or fear for God nor respect or consideration for man, Yet because this widow continues to bother me, I will defend and protect and avenge her, lest she give me intolerable annoyance and wear me out by her continual coming or/at the last she come and rail on me or/assault me or/strangle me. Then the Lord said, Listen to what the unjust judge says! And will not [our just] God defend and protect and avenge His elect (His chosen ones), who cry to Him day and night? Will He defer them and delay help on their behalf? I tell you, He will defend and protect and avenge them speedily.

This means that if you will work on your potentials, if you will just do what you need to do and work at it, the situation will bow. Go to the silver smith. When he puts the iron rod into fire and continues to hammer it, he has no doubt it will bend to the desired shape. Life will bend to your shape if you will give it the expected blow.

S—Serve God. The purpose of the parable about the widow and the judge is to describe the relationship between you and God. Jesus was simply telling the people how important it is that they serve the true God. Even Satan takes care of his servants. Human beings take care of themselves how much more, will the true God? Are you joking with eternity? Are you finding excuses not to serve the Most High God? Jesus says I am the Way, the Truth and the Life. My friend Sam Kputu wrote this on his blog. Thomas said to him, "Lord, we don't know where you are going, so how can we know the way?" Jesus answered, "I am the way, the truth and the life. No one comes to the Father except through me.—John 14:5, 6 [NIV] 'How dare you make such an outrageous claim; how could you say a minority religion like Christianity is superior to the numerous others that attract billions of followers . . . . that is bigotry 'This was the reaction of this young, innocent-looking, well-learned, upwardly mobile and obviously rich European as I sought to present the gospel and the claims of Jesus to him while waiting for our flight at a busy airport. The ferocity of his objection belied his gentle mien. I was left wondering why he was really offended, and thought of how to proceed with the discussion.

I soon came up with a Spirit-inspired answer. He had a laptop and an I-phone on him, so I politely asked him if he had a personal identification number (PIN) on both gadgets; he proudly answered 'yes'. I then asked if I could use my own PIN to access his gadgets, "there is no way except you are a hacker', he answered. I went on to ask him what right he had to decide that only one PIN could access his gadgets but the Lord of heaven and earth cannot enjoy the right to determine how He will be accessed."

T-Totally commit yourself. A great business leader[17] once said: ". . . the basic philosophy, spirit, and drive of an organization has far more to do with its relative achievements than do technological or economic resources, organizational structure, innovation, and timing. All these things weigh heavily in success. But they are, I think, transcended by how strongly the people in the organization believe in its basic precepts and how faithfully they carry them out." As true as this is for the success of a corporation, it is even more so for the individual. The most important single factor in individual success is commitment. Commitment ignites action. To commit is to pledge yourself to a certain purpose or line of conduct. It also means practicing your beliefs consistently. There are, therefore, two fundamental conditions for commitment. The first is having a sound set of beliefs. There is an old saying, "Stand for something or you'll fall for anything." The second is to have a faithful adherence to those beliefs with your behaviour. Possibly the best description of commitment is "persistence with a purpose". Meaning commitment and persistence are the two sides of a coin.

E—Encourage yourself and others. "*So David and his men came to the town, and behold, it was burned, and their wives and sons and daughters were taken captive. ⁴Then David and the men with him lifted up their voices and wept until they had no more strength to weep. ⁵David's two wives also had been taken captive, Ahinoam the Jezreelitess and Abigail, the widow of Nabal the Carmelite. ⁶David was greatly distressed, for the men spoke of stoning him because the souls of them all were bitterly grieved, each man for his sons and daughters. But David encouraged and strengthened himself in the Lord his God. I Sam 30:2-3 Amp*

The issue here is not just encouraging yourself, but how? David sought direction from God and got the necessary direction and pursued it. Good news he recovered all. God wants you to be encouraged and He has given you the means by which you can encourage yourself in Him.

1. Recognize that you do not have to stay discouraged. It may be like a bird that flies over your head, but you do not have to let it nest in your hair. You can be encouraged, and in fact, you can encourage yourself.

2. Remember that, if you know the Lord Jesus Christ, you are in covenant with God, and He has committed Himself to take care of you in every situation. When the circumstances of life pressed in on David, David pressed in on the benefits of his covenant relationship with God. He briefly outlined this in Psalm 103.

Bless the LORD, O my soul, and forget not all His benefits:

Who forgives all your iniquities,

Who heals all your diseases,

Who redeems your life from destruction,

Who crowns you with loving kindness and tender mercies,

Who satisfies your mouth with good things,

So that your youth is renewed like the eagle's

Stop giving voice to your discouragement and start giving voice to your encouragement. Stop repeating the lies of the devil and start speaking the promises of

God. Stop speaking out of fear and start speaking in faith. Stop talking about the problems and start talking about the solution. Find out what the Word of God has to say about your situation, then start speaking it, rather than your feelings.

4. Meditate on the LORD. One of the Hebrew words for "meditate" literally means to murmur, and implies the moving of the lips. Another word means to converse with yourself. It is your "self-talk," the way you speak to yourself about the things in your life. Everybody meditates on something, but often it is about the wrong thing, about the wrong person, or on the wrong focus.

You see, meditation is not a matter of positive thinking, and neither is encouragement. Rather, they are both matters of faith. It is not about us, but about Him. Let your meditation be about the Lord, about His love, His Word, His promises, His goodness, His works. As you do, you will be able to cast your cares on the Lord, with strong confidence that He cares about everything going on in your life (1 Peter 5:7).

We have thought, O God, on your loving kindness, in the midst of your temple. (Psalm 48:9)

But I will sing of your power; yes, I will sing aloud of your mercy in the morning; for you have been my defense and refuge in the day of my trouble. (Psalm 59:16)

I call to remembrance my song in the night; I meditate within my heart, and my spirit makes diligent search. (Psalm 77:6)

I will remember the works of the Lord; surely I will remember your wonders of old. I will also meditate on all your work, and talk of your deeds. (Psalm 77:11-12)

May my meditation be sweet to Him; I will be glad in the Lord. (Psalm 104:34)

I will meditate on your precepts, and contemplate your ways. I will delight myself in your statutes; I will not forget Your Word. (Psalm 119:15-16)

Oh, how I love your law! It is my meditation all the day. (Psalm 119:97)

My eyes are awake through the night watches that I may meditate on Your Word. (Psalm 119:148)

I remember the days of old; I meditate on all your works; I muse on the work of your hands. (Psalm 143:5)

I will meditate on the glorious splendor of your majesty, and on your wondrous works. (Psalm 145:5)

5. Get in the presence of the LORD. "Give thanks to the Lord. Enter his gates with thanksgiving and His courts with praise" (Psalm 104:4). This requires a quality decision: I will give thanks. I will praise.

Nehemiah said, "The joy of the LORD is your strength" (Nehemiah 8:10). David said to the Lord, "In Your presence is fullness of joy" (Psalm 16:11). When we get into the presence of the LORD we will find all the strength we need and encouragement for every circumstance.

6. Stand in the armor of God. Paul said, "Put on the whole armor of God, that you may be able to stand against the wiles of the devil." You can find a description of this in Ephesians 6:11-18:

We have the truth of God's Word, the righteousness of Christ and the gospel of peace (wholeness) at work on our behalf.

We have the helmet of salvation (salvation, healing, deliverance, prosperity and preservation) to guide and direct our thoughts.

We have the shield of faith to quench his fiery darts. Make no mistake, discouragement is most certainly one of the devil's fiery darts.

We have the sword of the Spirit, which is the Word of God. This is the offensive weapon that silences the voice of discouragement and all the lies of the devil.

We have all kinds of prayer in the Holy Spirit by which we can persevere and supply every need of the saints. Learn to pray as the Spirit of God leads.

Discouragement will tell you that you have nothing going for you and everything going against you. Encouragement tells you that you have everything going for you and it doesn't matter what you have going against you. God is on your side, with the provision for every need and the answer for every problem you may have. That is why Jesus came, and why, like David, you too can encourage yourself in the Lord your God.

N-No to evil life style. It must be made clear that **when** we are discoursing issue of persistence it must be persistence in noble causes not negative life styles. The widow did not go to bribe the judge. The widow did not come to seduce the judge. Recall the noble prayer of Jabez, it was not complete until the phrase 'and keep me from evil.' Paul in his great admonition that grace is superior to the law in the New Testament, quickly added 'can we continue in sin as say the grace of God should continue,' he answered the personal query 'God forbid!'. Even the judge said 'though I fear not God or regard any man, yet to prevent this woman from wearying me out I will avenge her.' The judge is therefore implying that even though he had a life style that could be regarded as less humanitarian or an evil life style that had no respect from God he could not continue in that life style. Look at the inference of Jesus Christ about the Judge '"And the Lord said, "Listen to what the unjust judge says. And will not God bring about justice for his chosen ones, who cry out to him day and night? Will he keep putting them off?" Jesus was also saying "will he keep putting them off". In other words will the God of heaven continue doing bad stuff? So you find that all the characters in this parable have a way of saying you cannot continue to live an evil life style.

We all know what it is to have a bad habit we hate but cannot stop. Some are merely annoying, and others can destroy the quality of our lives. Most of us struggle with at least one thing we do repeatedly that we detest but keep doing, even though the cost may be high. Whether it is procrastination or drinking too much, we do not fully own our lives.

The surest way to avoid bad habits sounds so simple, but here it is. Don't start! We make a thousand choices every day of our lives, and with many of those choices we have an opportunity to avoid establishing bad habits. The strength to make a life affirming choice comes from self-love and self-respect and often, respect for others.

When you were a child you may have grown up in an environment that made you believe you were bad, or unlovable, or not worthy. If this is so, then it is essential to do all you can to heal your self-esteem and find appreciation for yourself, in whatever ways you can. If you are currently raising children, you have the golden opportunity to instil in them high self-esteem so that they can resist the choices that lead to bad habits.

Many of the most destructive habits can be avoided altogether, if the strength to make a positive choice is there, like smoking. This is not a substance the body needs and it is easier to just never start. Self-esteem provides the power to say no to the peer pressure around. The same can be said of excessive drinking. If these habits are already in swing, then self-love and the motivation to be in charge of your life leads to seeking the support needed to take back your life from these bad habits.

A lot of people argue that the bad traits they have, were inherited from their parents and even grandparents. That is not a reason to continue in that life style. If you persist in that life style you are selling a bad life style to the future generation. Paul says if you continue indulging your flesh and do what he calls the works of the flesh you will not inherit the kingdom of God.: *"So I say, walk by the Spirit, and you will not gratify the desires of the flesh. ¹⁷ For the flesh desires what is contrary to the Spirit, and the Spirit what is contrary to the flesh. They are in conflict with each other, so that you are not to do whatever⁽ᶜ⁾ you want. ¹⁸ But if you are led by the Spirit, you are not under the law. ¹⁹ The acts of the flesh are obvious: sexual immorality, impurity and debauchery; ²⁰ idolatry and witchcraft; hatred, discord, jealousy, fits of rage, selfish ambition, dissensions, factions ²¹ and envy; drunkenness, orgies, and the like. I warn you, as I did before, that those who live like this will not inherit the kingdom of God."* Gal 5:16-18

C-Christ is the answer. The way to handle the issue of your life is to see Jesus Christ as your answer. I like this poem from Aaron Arubayi, *The Echos of the heart* that summarises how this happens:

The Lamb of God was crucified

Joycelyn Dankwa

The Lamb of God was buried
The Lamb of God was resurrected
The Lamb of God Paid for our salvation

The lion of the tribe of Judah
Wiped away our tears
The lion of the tribe of Judah
Restored boldness and confidence
Unto our fearful souls
The lion of the tribe of Judah
Is the shield and the fortress
Of our home
From the terrors that walketh in the night
Pity for the un-repentant heart

Unity, oneness, openness, love, hope, life
Accompanied his steps
Peace, jo, grace, mercy, compassion, forgiveness
Sorrows, worries, pains, frustration, hopefulness
Are in fight
Pity for the un-repentant heart

The long-night has delivered a redeemed beginning
The beginning was dedicated with song of eternity
The eternity of the life of joy unending
The joy of thankful merriment and celebrations
Pity for the un-repentant heart

Ah the lord of darkness has fallen
The king of glory has won the day
Satan and his household has fallen
Who say they do not deserve this fate?
Pity for the un—repentant heart

The lost and gone astray are bound for hell
The woods are now of unquenchable fire
The souls that sold themselves to Satan
Sinful souls are in eternal hell
Pity for the un-repentant heart

The condemned souls wailed for help
But hell is people with wicked spirits
The soul condemned says, Satan is my tormentor
Satan says but you of your own accord follow my heart
Pity for the un-repentant heart

The pathfinder finds us a path
The path leads to grace and salvation
The road-maker makes us a road
The road leads to life abundant in glory
Pity for the un-repentant heart

We should forget the past bruises
Out of the dreaded shadows of the night
We should live for kindness, mercy and forgiveness
Let the lord of death bury death unto death eternally
Pity for the un-repentant heart

O you living . . .
Pity for the souls that stand by
And watch,
While the wind of redemption
Passes by . . .

E-Energy is needed. Energy is needed to persist be it
spiritual, physical, emotional. There are many factors
which influence persistence as shared in the above

acronym of "PERSITENCE' but I believe discipline, vision and faith are the most influential of all but you need energy for these three critical factors. Discipline and persistence are habits worth forming. They can be manufactured through continued repetition, mindset and the Holy Ghost Power.

By making definite plans you remove the guesswork, guessing instead of knowing simply destroys persistence and sets you up for failure. There can be no room for doubt, fear and worry. Focus on the task in front, do not look left, do not look right and never look back, the past is in the past you cannot change it. Look forward, which is your future and make it what you want it to be, you can reach your goal if you have the faith and belief in yourself and persist.

The vision of your life must be big, big enough so that you will persist without exception. There is no way you can succeed without embracing this concept. Do not allow yourself to quit, you are only giving in to the fear and the worry and you will never win. Persistence is required despite exhaustion and when unforeseen obstacles are presented before you, despite thorough planning, you must remain strong, disciplined and focused. Persist and use it as an opportunity to be creative, use your imagination to find a different path. The anguish of learning is quickly forgotten when great results are achieved. Harness your willpower, look forward toward your goals, have the faith and belief in yourself, keep persisting and you will win. You deserve it.

CHAPTER FIVE

MULTIPLE LESSONS FROM THE PARABLE

The Story of the blind men and the Elephant

A version of this ancient the story says that six blind men were asked to determine what an elephant looked like by feeling different parts of the elephant's body. The blind man who feels a leg says the elephant is like a pillar; the one who feels the tail says the elephant is like a rope; the one who feels the trunk says the elephant is like a tree branch; the one who feels the ear says the elephant is like a hand fan; the one who feels the belly says the elephant is like a wall; and the one who feels the tusk says the elephant is like a solid pipe.

A king explains to them:

> "All of you are right. The reason every one of you is telling it differently is because each one of you touched the different part of the elephant. So, actually the elephant has all the features you mentioned."[1]

This resolves the conflict, and is used to illustrate the principle that truth can be stated in different ways. Jesus is the truth. Truth according to Dr Myles Monroe simply means the original. So many lessons could be learnt from the life of Jesus Christ more so from his parables the story of the importunate woman will surely not be different.

Jesus "was telling them a parable [the Unjust Judge] to show that at all times they ought to pray and not to lose heart. There was a widow in that city, and she kept coming to him, saying, 'Give me legal protection from my opponent.' For a while he was unwilling; but afterward he said to himself, 'Even though I do not fear God nor respect man, yet because this widow bothers me, I will give her legal protection, otherwise by continually coming she will wear me out.'"—Luke 18:1-5

This widow, by her persistence, was able to extract justice from this unmerciful judge. Jesus reasons "will not God bring about justice for his elect who cry to him day and night, and will he delay long over them? I tell you that he will bring about justice for them quickly."

How much more loving and just is God Almighty than a worldly judge! During times of trial, we should never give up and never stop praying. When Jonah was swallowed by a large fish, he prayed to God emphatically: "While I was fainting away, I remembered the LORD, and my prayer came to you, into your holy temple" (Jonah 2:7). God heard Jonah's prayer and delivered him from his great distress. When Jacob was afraid that his vengeful brother Esau would harm him or his family, he petitioned God: "Deliver me, I pray you, from the hand of my brother, from the hand of Esau; for I fear him, lest he come and smite [us all], the mothers with the children" (Genesis 32:11). God heard Jacob's prayer and softened the heart of his brother. Like Jonah, Jacob, and many other God-fearing, scriptural examples, we should have faith that God both hears and answers our prayers (Hebrews 11:6). When we face severe trials, let us persistently pray to God with heartfelt words, showing deep respect. Our loving heavenly father will hear us and come to the aid of his suffering children (Luke 11:13).

Among the parables, this one is signalized by the distinctness with which its object is announced at the commencement, and the principle of its interpretation at the end. No room is left here for diversity of opinion regarding the lesson, which the Lord intended to teach, or the manner in which the parable should be expounded. The design is expressed in verse first; the rule of interpretation in verses sixth and seventh. Why did the Master tell this story to his disciples? To teach them "that men ought to pray always, and not to faint." How may this lesson be derived from it? As the widow by her unremitting cry obtained her desire from the judge, God's own redeemed children will obtain from their Father in heaven all that they need, if they ask it eagerly, persistently, unwearyingly.

When we rightly comprehend the design of the parable, the difficulty connected with the bad character of the judge at once disappears. It was necessary to go to a corrupt tribunal in order to find a suitable case; a pure judgment seat supplies no such example. In certain circumstances, you might gather from a dunghill a medicinal herb which cleaner ground would never bear. The grain, which becomes our bread, grows best when its roots are spread in unseen corruption; and so perfect is the chemistry of nature, that the yellow ears of harvest retain absolutely no taint of the putrescence whence they sprung. Thus easily and perfectly the Lord brings lessons of holiness from examples of sin. He pauses not to apologize or explain: majestically the instruction advances, like the processes of nature, until the unrighteousness of man defines and illustrates the mercy of God.

It is not by accident,—it is by choice that this seed of the word is sown on filthy ground: it is sown there, because it will grow best there. The experience of a righteous human tribunal does not supply the material of this lesson. Where the presiding judge is just, a poor injured widow will obtain redress at once, and her perseverance will never be put to the test. The characteristic feature of the case which the Lord needed, was a persistent, unyielding perseverance in the cry for redress; for such a case he must go to a court where law does not regulate the judge, but where the judge for his own ease or interest makes his own law. The feature of Christ's teaching which most arrested intelligent listeners in his own day, was its inherent, self-evidencing majesty. Instead of seeking props, it stood forth alone, obviously divine. He taught with authority, and not as the scribes. Here is an example of that simple authority that is at once a witness to itself. He compares explicitly and broadly the method of God's dealing, as the hearer of prayer, with the practice of a judge who is manifestly vile and venal. Nor is a word of explanation or apology interposed. He who thus simply brings sweet food from noisome carrion, has all power in heaven and in earth; His ways are not as our ways, nor his thoughts as our thoughts.

As he needed for his purpose an example of judicial corruption, examples lay in human history; especially in the practice of oriental empires, ancient and modern, it is easy to find cases in which the supreme authority, civil and criminal, is vested in a deputy who habitually sacrifices justice to his own ease or interest.

The thorough evil of this judge, although stated distinctly, is stated briefly; it is not made prominent in the parable, and should not be made prominent in the interpretation of the parable. That evil on both sides, towards God and man, is I apprehend not introduced here for its own sake, but for the sake of a particular effect that resulted from it;—the frequent, persevering appeals of the widow for redress. This is the thing that is needed and used in the Lord's lesson; and although the injustice of the judge stands distinctly out on the face of the parable, it is like the forest tree in the vineyards of Italy, used only to hold up the vine. Earnest, repeated, unyielding appeal by a needy, feeble suppliant before the throne of power;—this is the fruit which is precious for the Teacher's purpose, and the hollow heart of the epicurean judge is employed only as the trunk to bear it. When it has held up that fruit to be ripened, itself may be thrown away.

At certain points in frequented routes through romantic scenery it is customary to fire a gun in order to afford the tourists an opportunity of hearing the echoes answering each other in the neighbouring mountains. The explosion is in a near place, in time first, and as to sound loudest, but this most articulate and arresting fact is employed exclusively for producing the subsequent and more distant echo. The explosion is instantly dismissed from the mind and attention concentrated on the reverberation which it called forth. The conduct of the judge in this parable stands precisely in the place of that explosion. When it has produced the widow's importunity it is of no further use; it must be thrown aside.

Let us hear now the interpretation,—"And the Lord said, Hear what the unjust judge saith," God's own chosen and redeemed people correspond to the suppliant widow in the parable. They are like her in her suffering and her weakness; they should be like her too in her non-intermittent, persevering cry.

Like other similar lessons, this one bears equally on the Church as a body, and on an individual Christian. The Church collective, in times of persecution, and a soul surrounded by temptations, stand equally in the place of the poor widow; they are in need and in danger. They have no resources in themselves; help must come from one that is mighty. It is their interest to plead with him who has all power in heaven and in earth,—to plead as men plead for life.

The lesson here is very specific; it bears on one point, and in order that all its force may be concentrated on one point, others are for the time being omitted. This parable is not spoken with the view of teaching that Christians ought to pray; that duty is assumed here, not enjoined. Neither does it prescribe what the suppliant should ask, or on whose merits he should lean. Taking for granted all these things which the Scriptures elsewhere explicitly teach, the Master in this lesson confines his attention to one thing,—perseverance in prayer when the answer does not come at first, perseverance and pertinacity, until the object is attained.

It is expressly intimated in the narrative that there is sometimes a long, and from our view-point inexplicable delay. This is the meaning of the expression "though he bear long with them." This phrase is not taken here in its ordinary significance,—an endurance of injuries; it means that he holds back long, and resists their pressure for relief.

Here are the two sides against each other: they cry day and night, and he, hearing their continuous cry, refrains from bestowing the relief for which they passionately plead. As God keeps back the answer, they redouble the cry; as they redouble the cry, God still withholds the answer. Expressly we are informed he will give answer; he will avenge his own elect. The eternal Father treasures up all the supplications of his children, and he will yet give them deliverance. When his time comes, the deliverance will be complete; but in the meantime, the interesting inquiry presents itself, why does he delay at all? In the light of Scripture we are able to give a satisfactory answer to this inquiry.

The reason why the widow's claims were left long unsettled in the court was the self-pleasing indolence of the judge. The love of his own ease was the motive that induced him both to refuse redress at first and to grant it afterwards. He refused to avenge her until he perceived that to do her justice would afford him less trouble than to withhold it. In the treatment which the petitions of the elect receive at the throne of God there is nothing in common with the conduct of the unjust judge, except the delay. The fact that the petitions lie for some time unanswered is common to both tribunals, but on all other points they are wholly diverse, and even the single feature of coincidence springs in the two cases from opposite grounds.

When God withholds the deliverance for which his children plead he acts with wisdom and love combined. It would be, so to speak, easier for a father who is at once rich and benevolent to comply immediately and fully with all the child's demands; it requires and exercises a deeper, stronger love to leave the child crying and knocking for a time in vain that the bounty given at the proper time may in the end be a greater boon. I once knew two men who lived near each other in similar worldly circumstances, but adopted opposite methods in the treatment of their children. The boys of this family obtained money from their father when they asked it, and spent it according to their own pleasure, without his knowledge or control: the boys of the other family often asked, but seldom received a similar supply. The father who frequently thwarted his children's desires loved his children more deeply, and as the result showed, more wisely than the father who could not summon courage sufficient to say no. The wise parent bore with his own when they pleaded for some dangerous indulgence, and the bearing wounded his tender heart; but by reason of his greater love, he bore the pain of hearing their cry without granting their request. The other parent was too indolent and self-pleasing to endure such a strain, and he lived to taste the bitter fruit from the evil seed which his own hand had sown.

For the same reason, and in the same manner, our Father in heaven bears with his own when they cry night and day to him for something on which their hearts are set. Because he loves us, he endures to hear our cry and see our tears. We do not certainly know what thorn penetrated Paul's flesh, but we know that it pained him much, that he eagerly desired to be quit of it, and that he besought the Lord thrice to take it away. From the fact that the child pleaded three times for the same boon, we learn that the Father bore with him awhile,—bore, so to speak, the pain of refusing, because he knew that the refusal was needful for Paul. The thorn was left in the flesh until its discipline was done, and then it was plucked out by a strong and gentle hand. "My grace is sufficient for thee:" there are no thorns in Paul's flesh now.

The case of the Syrophoenician[1] woman runs parallel with this as well as with the "Friend at midnight." Mark how the Lord bore with the woman. He delighted in her faith; it was his happiness to give, and yet he refused; in denying her he denied himself. But by withholding a while, he kindled her love into a brighter, stronger flame. By refusing what she asked, he reduplicated her asking; this is sweet to him and profitable to her. By the long delay on his part and the consequent eager repetition of the request on her part, a richer boon was prepared and bestowed. Her appetite was greatly quickened, and her satisfying was fuller. Who shall be filled most abundantly from the treasures of divine mercy at last? Those who hunger and thirst the most for these treasures in the house of their pilgrimage.

Think of the plainness of this lesson, and the authority that it possesses. Its meaning cannot be mistaken; we know what is spoken here, and we know who speaks. Hath he spoken, and shall he not make it good? The only begotten Son who is in the bosom of the Father, he hath declared him. Show us the Father, said Philip, and it sufficeth us; here Christ, in answer to his disciples' prayer, is showing the Father.

To reveal the Father's heart he spoke this parable. The helpless, needy woman came and came again, and cried, and would take no refusal, until the judge was compelled by her importunity to grant her request: and this is the picture chosen by the Lord Jesus when he desires to show how God regards suppliant disciples as they plead at his footstool. It is an amazing revelation, and the best of it is its truth. He who gave it has authority to speak. The Son will not misrepresent the Father; the Father's honour is safe in this Teacher's hands. We learn here, then, that the Hearer of prayer puts himself in the power of a suppliant. He permitted Jacob[2] to wrestle, and the firmer he felt the grasp the more he loved the wrestler. The words, "I will not let thee go except thou bless me," dropping in broken fragments from his lips at intervals as he paused and panted, were sweeter than angels' songs in the ears of the Lord of Hosts. He is the same still, as he is in the New Testament revealed by Jesus. The spirit in man that will take no denial is his special delight; the spirit that asks once and ceases he does away with. As the Lord loveth a cheerful giver, he loveth too an eager persevering asker. The door seems narrow, but its narrowness was not meant to keep us out; they please him best who press most heavily on its yielding sides. "The kingdom of heaven suffereth violence, and the violent take it by force[3]." The King of Glory feels well pleased with the warriors' onset,— and gladly welcomes the conqueror in.

It is indeed blessed to give: but the giver's blessedness is greatly marred by the listlessness of the needy creatures on whom he has bestowed his bounty. If they who need and get the goodness are insensible, and cold, and ungrateful, the joy of the benefactor is proportionally diminished. It is thus with "the giving God." When the receiver values the bounty, the delight of the bestower is increased. Thus the Lord Jesus was especially pleased as he healed the daughter of the Syro-Phoenician mother because she gave evidence by her importunity how much she valued the boon; and, on the other hand, his plaintive question, "Where are the nine[4]?" when the lepers took their cure so lightly, this shows that he did not much enjoy the act of healing because the diseased made light both of their ailment and their cure.

Come near, press hard, open your mouth wide, pray without ceasing; for this is the kind of asking that the great Giver loves. Unforgiven sin on the conscience keeps the sinful distant, and Satan calls the silence modesty. It is not; they most honour God who shows by their importunity in asking that they value his gifts.

While it is true that prayer should be a continuous fullness in the heart, ever pressing outward and upward, flowing wherever it can find an opening, it is not specifically that characteristic to which this parable points. This is not the lesson, "In everything by prayer and supplication, with thanksgiving, let your requests be made known unto God[5]:" the lesson here points not to the breadth of a whole spiritual life, but to the length of one line that runs through it. Whatever it be that a disciple desires, and is bent upon obtaining, he should ask not once, or twice, or twenty times, but ask until he obtains it; or until he dies with the request upon his lips: and in that situation, he will get his desire, and more. Trust in God: trust in his love. He who has not spared his own Son, how shall he not with him freely give us all things? Do not deem that delay is proof of his indifference. Delaying to bestow is not proof of indifference in God; but ceasing to ask is proof of indifference in man. Christ assures us he will give: that should induce us to continue asking.

While it is right to generalize the lesson, as we have already done, it is our duty also to notice the special form of the widow's prayer and the Lord's promise: in both cases it is vengeance against an adversary. The pleading is that the enemy who wronged the widow should be punished by the hand of power: the promise is that God will avenge his chosen ones, who cry to him.

The case is clearly one in which the weak are overpowered by an adversary too strong for them: unable to defend themselves, or strike down their foe, they betake themselves to God in prayer. The ailment is specific; such also is the request. Do justice upon this enemy—rid me of his oppression and his presence.

Ah, when a soul feels sin's power as a bondage, and sin's presence a loathsome defilement;—when a soul so oppressed flees to the Saviour for deliverance, the Lord will entertain the case, and grant redress. He will avenge. "The God of peace will bruise Satan under your feet shortly[6]."

No cry that rises from earth to heaven sounds so sweet in the ear of God as the cry for vengeance upon the enemy of souls. When there is peace between man and his destroyer, the closet is silent, and no groan of distress from the deep beats against the gate of heaven. This is not what Jesus loves. He came not to send this peace on earth, or in heaven; he came to send a sword. His errand was to produce a deadly quarrel between the captive soul and the wicked one, its captivator. When the cry rises, broken and stifled, but eager, as uttered by one engaged in deadly strife—when the cry, "Avenge me," rises from earth, God in heaven hears it and is well pleased. He delights when his people, hating the adversary of their souls, ask him for vengeance; and he will grant it. Long to the struggling combatant the battle seems to last, but speedily, according to God's just reckoning, the avenging stroke will fall. If there is delay it is but for a moment, and because this added moment of conflict will make the everlasting victory more sweet.

It is worthy of note, incidentally, that where an indolent judge, in order to avoid trouble, gives a just sentence to-day, he may, from the same motive, give an unjust sentence to-morrow. He who taught this lesson, knowing all that should befall himself, and hastening forward to his final suffering, knew well that deepest sorrow may spring from the selfishness of an unjust judge which happened for that time to bring deliverance to the widow. Pilate was precisely such a magistrate. Neither fear of God nor regard for man was the ultimate reason that determined his decision: the love of his own ease and safety was the hinge on which his judgment turned. He was disposed to do justly rather than unjustly in the case, when the Jewish rulers dragged Jesus to his bar. He would have pronounced a righteous judgment if that course had seemed to promise greater or equal advantage to himself. But the priests and people were, like this widow, very importunate and persevering. "Crucify him, crucify him," they cried. "Why, what evil hath he done?" "Crucify him, crucify him," rose again in a sound like the voice of many waters from the heaving throng. "Shall I release Jesus?" interposed the irresolute Pilate; "Away with this man, and give us Barabbas," was the instant reply. "Shall I crucify your king?" said Pilate, making yet another effort to escape the toils that were closing round him; but this fence laid him open to the heaviest blow of all: "If thou let this man go, thou art not Caesar's friend." He gave way at last: by their continual coming, they wearied him, and he abandoned the innocent to their will.

Thus the unjust as well as the just judgment seat has two sides. Jesus gave the safe side to the poor widow, and accepted the other for himself. He became poor that we might be rich: he was condemned that we might be set free.

CONCLUSION

In this book an attempt has been made to highlight some eternal values that could be distilled from two similar parables by the Lord Jesus Christ as recorded in Luke 18:1-8 and the similar one in Luke 11;5-8 (even though the emphasis was more on the former) is telling us about how the King of Kings wants us to face life's challenges, both from the ruler and the ruled.

Let me share another story with you from the Bible, comparing spiritual things with the spiritual. Let us compare parables with parables with the sole purpose that after you have read this book you will be far away from giving up a noble cause that God has given you, because there is a price awaiting you.

Once upon a time, a king had a great highway built for the people who lived in his kingdom. After it was completed, but before it was opened to the public, the king decided to have a contest. He invited as many of his subjects as desired to participate. The challenge was to see who could travel the highway the best and the winner was to receive a box of gold.

On the day of the contest, all the people came. Some of them had fine chariots; some had fine clothing and fancy food to make the trip a luxurious journey. Some wore their sturdiest shoes and ran along the highway on their feet to show their skill. All day they traveled the highway and each one as he arrived at the end, complained to the king about a large pile of rocks and debris that had been left almost blocking the road at one point, which had got in their way and hindered their travel.

At the end of the day, a lone traveler crossed the finish line wearily and walked over to the king. He was tired and dirty, but he addressed the king with great respect and handed him a small chest of gold. He said, "I stopped along the way to clear a pile of rocks and debris that was blocking the road. This chest of gold was under it all. Please have it returned to its rightful owner."

The king replied, 'You are the rightful owner'

"Oh no," said the traveler, "This is not mine. I have never known such money."

'Oh yes,' said the king, 'you have earned this gold, for you won my contest. He who travels the road best is not just the one that prays and persists but the one who makes the road better for those who follow.

1. We should never let unfavorable circumstances keep us from prevailing prayer. If this kind of importunate calling has such powerful effects in

relation to man, how much more with respect to God (James 5:16)!

2   We should use every legitimate argument possible with God, if honorable and with the proper motivation to have our desires met in Christ.

3. Importunate praying requires seeking those things that are "needful" (Luke 11:8). This man like the widow was not requesting a luxury; what he desired was not something optional, but obligatory.

4. The man and the widow went to the closest source he knew; someone with whom he was intimately acquainted. If anyone would help him in his time of need, it would surely be his friend.

5. This man came at an inconvenient hour and time midnight. While the neighbor was unhappy about the time, he reluctantly granted his request. There is never an hour inconvenient with God. The God who watches over his people neither slumbers nor sleeps (Psalm 121:3,4).

6. This man's own resources were exhausted. He had nothing to give of his own to the needy friend who had come seeking hospitality; "nothing to set before him."

We have nothing to give needy sinners of our own. If we would give them love, it is the love of Christ we must give them (II Corinthians 5:14); if it is truth, it is the truth of Christ we must present (John

14:6); spiritual manna is the manna from heaven (John 6:35) which we must share. That which we would give to meet the needs of others is only that which God has freely given to us.

7. These parables do not teach that prayer is an enforcement of ourselves into God's presence, or the wringing of something from a reluctant God. They are studies in contrasts. "If a bad man (or an indifferent friend will yield to the mere force of an importunity, which he hates, how much more will a righteous God be prevailed upon by the powerful prayer which he loves"

EPILOGUE

Limitation is the function of our perception. Know that your sky is not the limit. Your life is as lonely as you like to make it to be. Your joy is as much as you decide to feel, your right is as long as you decide to make it. No one sets the limits for you but you with the help of God. No one can stretch the span of the sky as you. All you need to do is rise with determination; spread your wings like an eagle and soar to the top where you belong; yes you can. If an egg is broken due to outside force then life ends. If it breaks from the inside; life begins. Great things always begin from the inside.

Brighten up and respond to the art of genius in you. A successful person has the art of building a house with the stones that others have thrown at him. So turn every rejection to a solid direction. Let every stumbling block become a stepping stone to greatness. I pray that God will turn your

- Test to a testimony
- Trial to triumph
- Mess to a message
- Gory to glory
- Breakdown to a breakthrough
- Pain to gain

I know lines are falling unto you in pleasant places; yea you have a godly heritage psalm 16;6

Think about this when a snake is alive, the snake eats ants. When a snake dies ants eat the snake. Time can turn things around so beware how you treat people. Don't neglect anyone one on earth. Let your investment count for eternity.

Receive the grace of smile and enjoy a life full of vitality. Know that the joy of thy Lord is your strength. Bubble with a life of excitement today and always. Tap into the wonder of smiling without any price tag. Do you know it takes 73 muscles to frown and 14 to smile. No wonder grouchy people are always tired. It has been said if you laugh everyday it is equal to ten minutes of exercise. I appeal to you, laugh today and in your journey of life no matter the circumstances, laugh sufficiently and you will be healthy without drugs. Position yourself for new day, and new blessings. Don't let yesterday's failure ruin the beauty of today, the blessings of God are new everyday morning. Today has its own promises of love, forgiveness joy and success. Tap into it. May you be the show piece of his masterpiece. It is well in the mighty name of Jesus.

Your life is not a function of the obstacles you face but your attitude to overcome through thanks giving. Life without thanksgiving is boring and dull. Hope without thanksgiving frustrates God's purposes. Faith without thanksgiving robs of strength and fortitude, to enjoy prosperity and longevity. The great book says. In all things give thanks . . . even in tears it shall be well.

Life is like music. It has high notes and low notes. No matter how high or low your notes may be, keep in tune with God and you will never go out of tune in the music of life. Hosea 12:13 says, and by a prophet the Lord brought Israel out of Egypt, and by a prophet was he preserved. So by prophecy today; your dream will be granted. So flow now in the prophecy of God's glory unto greatness for your life, and you'll see the goodness of thy Lord in the land of the living. Amen.

Bible References And Biblography

Preface
Chapter One
I Samuel 30:1-6
James 1:27
Eccl 11:3a
Heb 11:11
2Pet 1:9
Isaiah 40:4
Ex 23:26

Chapter 2 http://www.cybernation.com/victory/youcandoit/neverquit.php

Chapter 3
Joshua 1: 8
Heb 11:32
http://www.abanet.org/publiced/volunteer/judge_whatdo.html
Esther 3

Psalm 1
http://www.abusivelove.com/AbusiveLove_2_0.htm
http://www.poems-and-quotes.com/author_quotes.
html?id=317925
Isaiah 53and John 1
Isaiah 1:18
http://health.ecynosure.com/uncategorized/
what-is-frustration
Kings 4: 1-2

Matthew 23:14
I Cor 10:13
Chapter four
Genesis 1:2
Genesis 12: 4-9
Genesis 16,Heb 11:11
Romans 8:9
Psalm 92:10
James 2:14-26
Luke 10:17-24
Luke 10:23-29
Romans 9:30-33.
Romans 2:18
Matthew 5:45.
Proverbs 228
Jer 17;11
Jas 3:17
Acts 3
Lk 18:6-8
Thomas J. Watson, Jr., *A Business and its Beliefs—The ideas that helped build IBM*

Chapter five
Matthew 15:21-28
Gen 32
Matthew 11:12
The story of the ten lepers
Phil 4:6
The God of peace will bruise Satan under your feet
shortly[6]